the ARCHANGELS *and the* ANGELS

TARAJYOTI GOVINDA

The Archangels and the Angels
© G. A. Govindamurti 1999

Published by:
Deva Wings Publications
P.O. Box 200
Daylesford, Victoria, Australia
www.devawings.com

National Library of Australia
Cataloguing-in-Publication details as follows:

Govinda, Tarajyoti 1958-1999
The archangels and the angels

ISBN 978-0-9587202-2-9
1. Angels. 2. Spiritual life. 1. Title.

291.215

This book is dedicated to

Ananda Tara Shan

for her love and dedication

to the Lord Maitreya

and the spiritual Cause

CONTENTS

FOREWORD

In 1984, during a death experience, I made contact with the angels. They came as messengers of the Glory of God, letting me know I should not despair, nor sink into a state of hopelessness. They revealed the power of Light and Love and helped me find that power within myself. That experience and vision has remained with me to this day. Since then, I have had countless other experiences which have served to re-awaken me to the glory of the angels and their work for the Earth and humanity. These experiences stimulated me to write my first two books, *The Language of the Heart: is spoken all over the world* and *The Healing Hands of Love: a guide to spiritual healing.*

Through the work of my Teacher, Ananda Tara Shan, through her teachings and Earth healing services, I have come to know and understand much about the Archangels, who guide and inspire the work of the angels as they work to uplift us in Light. Though there is some information about the Archangels in print, I have found a lack of literature that provides information about all the Archangels and the angels in one volume. I also find the language used in some of the literature is not conducive to the common reader. I have therefore endeavoured in this book to provide a text that provides an easy-to-read account that tells about who the Archangels and the angels are, what they do, and, where this was possible, to describe the characteristics of specific Archangels and angels that are known. *The Archangels and the Angels* is based on personal knowledge and experience, clairvoyance and theosophical literature, such as the work of Geoffrey Hodson, H.P. Blavatsky, Annie Besant and C.W. Leadbeater. It also includes information from Corinne Heline's book *Stargates*.[1] I feel that people should know about the Archangels and the angels. In this way we can better cooperate with them, raise the consciousness of humanity and help relieve the world crisis affecting humanity and the Earth.

ARCHANGELS

THE ARCHANGELS

According to Blavatsky,[2] an Archangel is "the highest supreme angel." In theosophical terms, the Archangels are at the head of the angel evolution. They are Mighty Beings who wield mighty forces of Light at cosmic levels as they have evolved into cosmic consciousness. They are known as the "Seven Mighty Spirits before the Throne".[3] The Archangels wield cosmic energy and imbue original matter with cosmic Light. This creates an evolutionary impulse on Earth.[4]

The Seven Mighty Spirits before the Throne are the Archangels Michael, Jophiel, Chamuel, Gabriel, Raphael, Uriel and Zadkiel. There are also seven female Archangels who are their twin rays. These are the Lady Archangels: Faith, Constance, Charity, Hope, Mary, Donna Grace and Amethyst. The female Archangels have a strong role, standing beside the male Archangels to create a united force.

The Archangels shape the solar system according to the Divine idea. They work ceaselessly to serve the Christ, and assist Him in his mission to transmute and transform all planet life on Earth with Divine Love, Divine Intelligence, and Divine Will. They bring Spirit into matter, creating the kingdom of God upon the Earth. The Archangels cooperate with each other, and are alert to the task. In this way they are supported by their armies of Light-workers to fulfil their tasks in the Plan. They remain loyal and devoted to the task. The task is to assist the Christ in the unfoldment of the Plan, to do whatever He asks. It is their cooperation and ability to serve that enables the Christ to rely upon these Beings to carry out the work, and the Plan itself can unfold.

Their unified cooperation and loyalty to the task achieves the needed purpose of protecting the Earth, supplementing and supporting Michael's work of defending the faith and the unified vision, which enables the Earth and humanity to be touched and transformed by the Light of the Christ. Each Archangel can rely on the others to supplement and support His or Her work. We can learn from their example to better serve the Hierarchy and fulfil the Plan. They stand at each corner of the Earth, protecting the Earth and all life on it, through this cooperative effort.

All the Archangels wield mighty forces of Light, impregnating higher vibrations of the Christ Light into the planet Earth and all Light Beings, who are active and alert to fulfil their needed tasks in the Plan. The hierarchical structure of the Angelic kingdom is a needed and incredible Plan that leaves no detail out. It brings new life and hope of a Christed world. The Light-workers, fairies, angels and devas alike need those more evolved to assist them to become Christed. The Angelic kingdom is like one organism. When the Archangels are at work, everything takes place in perfect harmony, as in a symphony played by an orchestra. Through that action, the sound of the Christ is heard and the words of God are spoken. The role of the Initiate, a person who is very advanced spiritually and who has three or four initiations in their soul, is to be the vehicle, the vessel through which God's words can come. The Archangels, the angels and the Initiates become transformers through which the Mighty Light and Power of God can come to us.

The Archangels want us to know about them. They want us to treat them with the right honour, love, and respect and to start to open the channels between the human kingdom and the Angelic kingdom. As we do this they can help us. They have the key to how we can develop and create the Kingdom of God on Earth. They are prepared to give this key to the pure of heart. We have to develop the yearning in our hearts and aspire towards the Divine Light. When we purify ourselves enough the knowledge can be given. Through the work of the Archangels it is possible that we open to the birth of Christ in our hearts. The Archangels, with their varying armies of Light, will help us to work towards the unfoldment of the Divine Plan, find what we need to know, and support actions that are of Light. They have millions of messengers at their command. We can ask for help from these Angels and they will help, according to our karmic condition and grace.

The Archangels bring the energy and qualities of the Seven Rays, according to the Ray they are on. The Seven Rays are Mighty Cosmic Entities Who wield streams of cosmic Light which contain pure qualities and energy of a very high vibration that come from the Solar Logos. Each Ray brings forth particular qualities. The Archangels can often take on the colour of the Ray they bring to us. They may also appear bringing forth other colours. See Table 1 for the colour, Archangels and qualities associated with each Ray. To understand about the colours of Angels, we look to the Ray that the Angel or Archangel comes on. (See Table 1). Generally these Beings of Light take on the colour of the Ray on which they work. It doesn't mean that they can't be seen emanating and giving life-force to other colours. The Archangels are beyond colour, yet they bring colour to us. Gabriel appears in many paintings of the Annunciation, for example, that by Leonardo De Vinci, and one by Millozo Delfourly. Gabriel's main colour is blue, yet in paintings of Gabriel it is possible to find some violet, some light blue, some white, some gold, some green. It is difficult to show how beautiful the Archangels are, and to capture their magnificence. They are mighty Beings with mighty wings, leading all other angelic Beings, from great devas to tiny fairies which go around in our gardens. The Archangels send their mighty forces of Light, bringing different colour and different energies through their loyal servers in the Angelic Kingdom. These majestic and very powerful forces of Light are sent to Earth to help us and to guide us. Certain music helps us to tune into the Archangel energies.

We need to visualise the angels at work and be aware of them in daily life to help us cooperate better with the Plan. We need to make friends with these Beings, to respect, honour, and open communication between the Angelic and human kingdoms, developing love between these worlds, so that humanity and the Earth can gain entrance into these higher worlds. If we know which of the Archangels are involved in certain activities, it helps to call upon them and their legions of angels to help us to do that work. We can do so in the privacy of our own homes, when we do our meditations, or in Earth Healing Services where we may work as a group. By calling upon the Archangels, we open up the channels of communication between the human kingdom and the Angelic kingdom.

TABLE 1. THE ARCHANGELS AND THEIR RAY

Ray	Colour(s)	Archangel	Lady Archangel	Qualities
1	Electric Blue Fiery Red White	Michael	Faith	Will of God
2	Golden Yellow Azure Blue	Jophiel	Constance	Love, Wisdom
3	Emerald Green Pink	Chamuel	Charity	Active Intellegence
4	White Royal Blue	Gabriel	Hope	Harmony via conflict, Purity, Beauty
5	Olive Green Dark Blue	Raphael	Mary	Love with Purpose, Concrete science and knowledge
6	Majestic Red	Uriel	Donna Grace	Devotion, Self-sacrifice
7	Violet	Zadkiel	Amethyst	Law and Order, Transformation, Freedom

WHAT IS THE DIFFERENCE BETWEEN AN ARCHANGEL AND A MASTER?

An Archangel and a Master come from two different kingdoms of evolution. A Master is a great Being Who has walked the Earth and Who has perfected Him- or Herself throughout incarnations of Earthly existence until they reached Mastership (perfection). They are perfected souls who have become one with the Law of God. They no longer need to embody. They work on the inner planes and do great work on the inner planes, serving the Christ. Because they are working on the inner planes, many of the Masters have an Archangelic inner form which they work through. They can be seen in Their Archangelic form on the inner, with great wings wielding mighty forces of Light. They therefore work closely with the Archangels in cooperative effort for the Christ.

An Archangel is a great Being Who evolves through the Angelic evolution, which is a completely separate evolution to that of the human kingdom. The Archangels are at the head of the angelic evolution. If we take Lady Mary as an example we see that it is possible to be both a Master and an Archangel. She is both a Lady Master and a Lady Archangel. During different stages of her evolution She has evolved through both the human and the angelic kingdom.

WHAT DO THE ARCHANGELS DO?

The Archangels and their armies of Light beings work in cooperation, assisting Michael in bringing forth God's Plan for the Earth. Archangel Michael helps us to be aware of that Plan. He works to protect the forces of good from the forces of evil, so that the Plan may unfold, according to the Love and Will of God, the Father-Mother. Archangel Gabriel has often been asked to warn against disasters. Archangel Michael has also done this, as have Raphael and Uriel. We can call upon the Archangels to answer our prayers and to send healing to the sick, the suffering, to those in need, and to where it is needed the most on Earth. Archangel Raphael, through his legions of angels, sends healing to humanity, helping us to heal our deep, inner wounds. He works to heal humanity and clear away the debris after disasters and events of human error, working often with Archangel Mary, bringing calm after the storm. The White Tara, a Cosmic Being who also has an Archangelic form, is also very active in the role of Light-bringer. The female Archangels and the White Tara have a strong role, standing beside the male Archangels to create a united Force. Lady Nada, a female Master (a great Being who has mastered spiritual life through the human evolution) can send a healing angel to those in need. It is within the Law to ask that others may be helped by these angels until they are made well. Donna Grace, the female Archangel on the sixth Ray, works to bring grace to all who need and are deserving of it. Archangel Uriel works ceaselessly to heal and bless the

Earth and all life on it with the Light of God. Uriel's major work is that of Earth healing. He sends his armies of Light to help heal the Earth, the Earth's atmosphere and the ozone layer. At such times when the negative actions of humanity affect the Earth itself, for example, during nuclear testing, Uriel and his armies work ceaselessly to counteract what is enabled by the prayers of some of humanity and the Will of God.

Gabriel helps us to expand our consciousness of Love beyond those we have affection for to include even our enemies. This broadened Love moves to include every race and creed. It has within it genuine appreciation of the Divine Essence in all, however imperfect all may be. His message of love is that of true brother/sisterhood. He shows how all division and separateness must be resolved into unity, until there are no conflicting nations and races. As the New Testament[5] states, "Abideth Faith, Hope and Love: the greatest of these is Love." This is the message and purpose of the Christ, to unite all people, all nations, and all religions within His Loving Heart. This is the Great Plan towards which all the Archangels are working.

Let us look at the Archangels individually, in a little more depth, according to their particular Ray.

INDIVIDUAL ARCHANGELS AND THEIR ROLES

In this section the term twin ray is used to explain the relationship between some of the male and female Archangels. Twin ray refers to the fact that these particular Archangels have a very close relationship, due to their mutual origin from the same spark of life force sent forth by the Solar Logos, or God. In the beginning of the creation of Spirits also known as Monads, God, the Solar Logos, sends forth a stream of life or a Spark of God. Within that one spark or stream there are many life-streams which are divided and which develop into a two-fold structure manifesting as a masculine life-stream and a feminine life-stream. The term twin ray refers to the masculine or feminine counterpart who is the other half of the spark of God that each one shares.

RAY 1

THE LORD ARCHANGEL MICHAEL

The Lord Archangel Michael is the protector of the Christ and defender of the Faith. He protects all who work for the Light. He is known as the Prince of All Angels, the Archangel of Protection, the Prince of Angelic Hosts, the Lord of the Archangels, the Director of the Angelic Kingdom, the Angel of Deliverance, the Great Prince, the Prince of the Church, the Dragon Slayer, Christ's Ambassador and the Founder of the Mysteries.[6] He is often seen with the Sword of Truth in his right hand. The sword has become the symbol most commonly associated with Michael. The Scales of Justice are another symbol associated with Michael as he stands for Justice and all that is good. As the dragon-slayer he fights against the forces of darkness and He is the Archangel we call on when we need protection. With the help of His sword we can free ourselves from the darker forces both within and around us. Michael and His legions of angels, which are commonly referred to as Michael's army, work constantly that Light may prevail and help all who seek to live in the Light to do so, unharmed by the dark forces which invade in our hours of weakness and despair. Archangel Michael played a major role in the Arthur legends, and with St. Joan d'Arc. (See the Four Archangels of the Stargates later in the next chapter for more information on Michael.)

LADY FAITH

Lady Faith stimulates the quality of faith within us. In so doing she helps us to keep faith in the Christ and in the unfoldment of the Divine Plan. She works closely with the Archangel Michael and is His twin ray. She is also working to stimulate an aspect of the three-fold flame in our heart centres. The colours of the three-fold flame are blue, gold and rose-coloured. Each flame contains certain qualities we need to help us link to our soul and Spirit. Lady Faith holds the energy of the blue flame of faith within the three-fold flame. By calling on the three-fold flame in our hearts we lift in vibration in a way that will help us to manifest more Spirit in our lives. We let our Christ-self know that we wish to align ourselves towards it.

LADY MARY

Lady Mary is well known for her perseverance and determined will. She remains fixed at her post until her task is complete. Though she works still with her twin ray Archangel Raphael on the fifth Ray, much of her work has moved to the first Ray to assist the Avatar of Will, who is working to bring the energy of the Will of God to Earth and humanity. (An Avatar is a Cosmic Being who embodies a purpose or quality to serve God's Plan on Earth.) Lady Mary brings the understanding of freedom of heart and shows us how when we truly follow our hearts we open to the will of God in our lives.

RAY 2

ARCHANGEL JOPHIEL

Archangel Jophiel brings great joy, love and wisdom and helps us to bear our suffering. The joy He brings is the joy of soul. He helps us to understand our suffering and to see its necessity for the opening of our hearts. We can find Him in our hearts.

LADY CONSTANCE

Lady Constance brings to us the quality of constancy. She can stimulate that quality within our hearts to help us remain in alignment with the higher forces of love and Light. She works closely with Archangel Jophiel and is His twin ray.

RAY 3
ARCHANGEL CHAMUEL

Archangel Chamuel is the Archangel of Adoration. His colour is pink. We can call to Him to help us align to our soul and Spirit. Archangel Chamuel sends forth the Light of the Holy Spirit.

LADY CHARITY

Lady Charity brings the energy of forgiving love, the inner expression of love and love of life. Her charity prevents the action of discord. She is also working to stimulate the charity aspect of the three-fold flame in our heart centres, with Lady Hope and Lady Faith stimulating the qualities of hope and faith, respectively.

RAY 4

ARCHANGEL GABRIEL

Archangel Gabriel is the Messenger of Love; impersonal, all-embracing love that melts separatism through unity, that is " Spirit Love winged with celestial force"[7] and is based on a genuine appreciation of the Divine Essence in all. His name means Hero of God. He is aware of the Divine Plan. He awakens the feeling of the reality of the Christ-Self within us and helps us to become one with it. He uses the Christ Light to purify, elevate and spiritualise souls. He also works on planetary purification. He is often seen with the lily as the symbol of purity and in pictures of the Immaculate Conception.

In the process of birth, Gabriel brings blessing and counsel to all who will incarnate in the coming year as they come into the etheric region prior to being born into the physical world. His legions of angels guide souls through the etheric region and he oversees this process.

Gabriel is the Archangel of Revelation. He is said to have foretold the destruction of the Persian empire by Alexander the Great. He is also said to have told Zacharias he would become the father of John the Beloved, was the Angel of the Annunciation, announced the birth of Samson to his mother, comforted Jesus in the garden of Gesthemane, and is revered in Islam because he dictated the Koran to Mohammed.[8]

He had a major role as teacher and counsellor to Lady Mary, and in the mission of Jesus and the Path of love and service. He reveals the Nativity Mysteries, the Way of Initiation, of becoming Christed. He is nurturer of activities throughout nature[9]. (See the Four Archangels of the Stargates later in the next chapter for more information on Gabriel.)

LADY HOPE

Lady Hope brings the quality of hope which turns us around and sets us on the Path, changing the most discordant conditions into a life of new and joyful experience. Hope is a spiritual reality, and it redeems the dragon (our lower nature). Hope is eternal and is ever-present in even our darkest hours. The hope is that we may proceed into higher Light. Hope lives deep within us. She works from the Temple of Resurrection with Gabriel, giving the feeling of expectancy and upliftment. A Ray of Her quality is implanted within our life essence. She can intensify it and thus raise our hope to assist the Christ-Self to fulfil the Divine Plan. She works with Lady Faith and Lady Charity to stimulate the three-fold flame in our heart centres.

RAY 5
ARCHANGEL RAPHAEL

Archangel Raphael is the Archangel of healing, bringing comfort and mercy to those who suffer and are in need. He has legions of angels at his command, dedicated to helping humanity and the Earth and to acting on any mission the Christ wishes. He has trained in nature with the focus of concentration. (See the Four Archangels of the Stargates later in the next chapter for more information on Raphael.)

LADY MARY

Lady Mary is the twin ray of Archangel Raphael. She played a major role as the mother and vision-holder for the Lord Jesus and His mission, and is working now closely both with Raphael and the Avatar of Will. She has trained with Raphael and Gabriel in the work of concentration in the nature temples. Raphael and Gabriel would often visit and assist her even as a child, preparing her for her mission with Jesus. At the time of Jesus' resurrection she became the cosmic mother for humanity. According to Luk,[10] she carried on the work in Bethany for the next thirty years or more, and travelled to Ireland, Crete, Britain and France to establish foci of Light.

Mary is an Archangel and so also commands legions of angels to assist her in her work. We have looked at her work on the first Ray.

RAY 6

ARCHANGEL URIEL

The brilliance and beauty of the Archangel Uriel, the Light of God, Angel of Vision and Beauty, comes on the sixth Ray, working closely with Master Jesus and Lady Nada. He is the interpreter of the prophecies, the Angel of Retribution and Salvation. He heals the Earth and dispenses spiritual Light, with vision and beauty as keynotes. He opens vision by slow degrees.[11] He reveals the mysteries of transformation, ascension and alchemy. The Sermon on the Mount was given during his reign. "Blessed are the peacemakers for they shall inherit the Earth[12]." Uriel was said to have warned Noah of the impending deluge[13]. He is said to have disclosed the mysteries of the heavenly world to Ezra, interpreted prophecies and lead Abraham out of Ur. According to Heline,[14] Uriel, together with Gabriel, transmits the currents from Sirius.

The energy of Sirius is behind the Christ, and it is this energy which has the capacity to transform planet life. Uriel works in the Earth's atmosphere, penetrating the core of the Earth with the Christ Light. Through Him, physical activities reach their zenith. He acts on people's prayers, sending his angels to heal the Earth. (See the Four Archangels of the Stargates later in the next chapter for more information on Uriel.)

DONNA GRACE

Donna Grace and Lady Nada assist Uriel in helping send healing angels to minister to Earth and humanity. Donna Grace, Uriel's twin ray, is the representative of grace in the angelic kingdom in a similar way that Mary represents grace to humanity. She is able to intensify the energy of grace in us when we call on her. She can help us to get through troubled times. We can call on Donna Grace to help us find the Grace of God. It is sent as a feeling of grace, a feeling that we can move on, we can let go and open to a new path and a new way.

RAY 7

ARCHANGEL ZADKIEL

Archangel Zadkiel guards the powers of invocation and keeps invocation pure and in Light. His energy acts as a protection to invocations. This is how he serves the Christ, keeping pure and transmuting any negativity.

LADY AMETHYST

Lady Amethyst holds the energy of the creative intelligence within the violet Ray, the Mother aspect. She is the twin ray of Zadkiel. She is strongly connected with work in the mineral kingdom through the amethyst crystal.

the ARCHANGELS *and the* SEASONS

THE ARCHANGELS AND THE SEASONS

The commencement of the four sacred seasons - winter, spring, summer and autumn - commencing at the two equinoxes and the two solstices, mark the four gates through which the Cosmic Christ makes contact with the Earth. The Cosmic Christ, simply stated, is the life essence of the Sun itself, a Cosmic Being of great potence. Thus He is also referred to as Sun Spirit. The four sacred seasons are expressions of principal events of the life of the Cosmic Christ. The solstices occur on the 22nd of December (the winter solstice in the northern hemisphere) and the 22nd of June (the summer solstice) each year. The equinoxes occur on the 21st of March (the spring equinox in the northern hemisphere) and the 23rd or 24th of September (the autumn equinox) each year. Esoterically, the solstices and equinoxes are times when, if we meditate and attune ourselves to the higher forces, our potential for clarity of contact with those forces is heightened. Thus, many in esoteric circles come together for meditation and services at these times. As at the times of the full moon, there is a heightened awareness of Spirit.

The equinoxes and solstices are referred to as "stargates." They mark the time when the Archangels change their reign. During the equinoxes and solstices, in all seasons, the Masters of Wisdom give the needed spiritual teachings to the world, and assist us along on the Path of spiritual evolution.

THE FOUR ARCHANGELS OF THE STARGATES

During the four seasons, the Archangels Michael, Raphael, Gabriel and Uriel reign, symbolising the Path of Initiation, leading through Birth, Crucifixion, Resurrection and Ascension. Each of these Archangels is associated with a particular "stargate".[15] In Table 2 we see the equinox or solstice, the astrological period and the degree of the path of Initiation associated with each of these four Archangels.

In Figure 1 we see that these four Archangels are seated at the Throne of God.

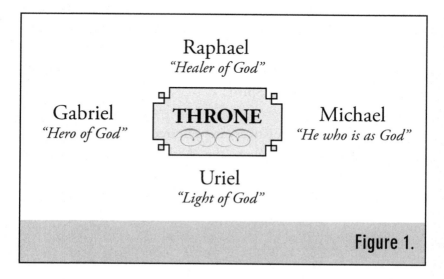

Figure 1.

TABLE 2.

Archangel	Equinox/ Solstice	Astrological Period	Degrees of the Path of Initiation
Michael	Autumn	♎ Libra ♏ Scorpio ♐ Sagittarius	the Crucifiction
Gabriel	Winter	♑ Capricorn ♒ Aquarius ♓ Pisces	the Holy Birth
Raphael	Spring	♈ Aries ♉ Taurus ♊ Gemini	the Resurrection
Uriel	Summer	♋ Cancer ♌ Leo ♍ Virgo	the Ascension

STARGATE 1

Archangel Michael is linked with the autumn equinox of the northern hemisphere. In the southern hemisphere this is the spring equinox. This time esoterically is associated with the Crucifixion of the Cosmic Christ. At this time, the Cosmic Christ binds Himself to the cross of matter, sacrificing Himself for us.

STARGATE 2

The Archangel Gabriel is linked with the northern winter solstice. In the southern hemisphere this is the summer solstice, celebrated at Christmas. This time esoterically is associated with the Holy Birth. At this time the Christ Light reaches the inmost center of the globe, impregnating all with Light.

STARGATE 3

The Archangel Raphael is linked with the spring equinox in the northern hemisphere. This is the autumn equinox in the southern hemisphere. This time esoterically is associated with the Resurrection of the Sun Spirit. The Cosmic Christ is liberated from the cross of matter and returns to the heavenly world of our Mother-Father God.

STARGATE 4

The Archangel Uriel is linked with the summer solstice in the northern hemisphere. This is the winter solstice in the southern hemisphere. This time esoterically is associated with the Ascension of the Cosmic Christ. The Cosmic Christ renews His life spirit and is born again in his own home world.[16]

The four Archangels have particular colours, elements and symbols associated with them. Their names also have meaning (see Table 3).

The seasons in which the four Archangels reign are associated with specific signs of the zodiac.

See Figure 2a-d (pages 34-35) to find the associated signs of the zodiac.

TABLE 3.

Archangel	Colour	Element	Symbol	Meaning of name
Michael	Blue Red (Fiery)	Fire	the sword	He who is as God
Gabriel	Blue	Water	the lily	Hero of God
Raphael	Green	Air	the grail	Healer of God
Uriel	Majestic Red	Earth	celestial blossoms	Light of God

Even though particular Archangels are in the main office during the four different seasons, the other Archangels are still working ceaselessly. All Archangels play their roles at the solstices and equinoxes and particularly at Christmas time, when there is major movement in terms of initiation for humanity. The Archangels work together at the times of these major festivals. On the path of the aspirant, these four festivals of the year give purification and transmutation, leading the aspirant eventually to the Path of the disciple. The aspirant is admitted into the temple by the Archangel Uriel, who guards the gate. The aspirant then comes into the presence of Gabriel

> *who greets the new disciple as 'the son of the star,'*
> *the name by which the Christ initiates have been*
> *known, ever since the Holy Mysteries were first*
> *founded by Michael in Atlantis millennia ago.*
> (Heline[17])

Let us look at the four Archangels in greater detail.

ARCHANGEL MICHAEL

Archangel Michael comes into his reign at the autumn equinox in the northern hemisphere. As said earlier, this time esoterically is a time of crucifixion where the Christ is again sending His energies to help bring harmony to the discord on this planet. There is nothing so beautiful and

FIGURE 2A.
    AUTUMN EQUINOX & MICHAEL'S REGIN

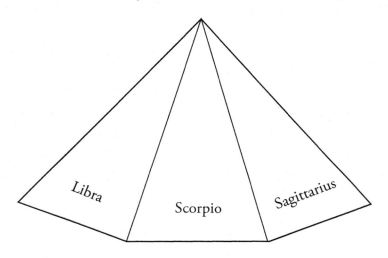

FIGURE 2B.
    WINTER SOLSTICE & GABRIEL'S REIGN

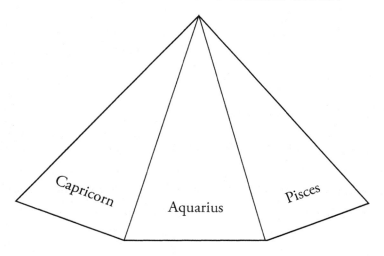

FIGURE 2C.
   SPRING EQUINOX & RAPHAEL'S REGIN

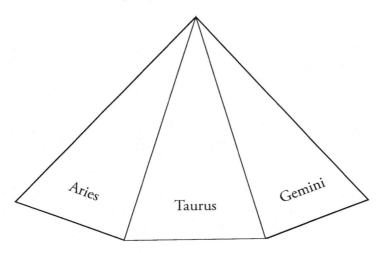

FIGURE 2D.
   SUMMER SOLSTICE & URIEL'S REIGN

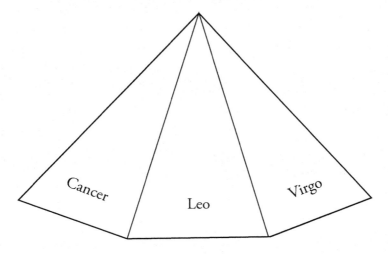

majestic as the sight of Archangel Michael who comes to protect the Christ in this process. He can be seen arriving with enormous strength as defender of the faith, sword in hand, sometimes pictured on a horse. He is among the oldest of beings on this Earth and has been here since the beginning of time. Under the influence of Michael, the pure of heart are found. They are incorruptible and cannot be bribed. He has legions of angels at His command and sits at the top of the scheme second only to the Christ Himself. There are millions of angels beneath Him of all kinds ready to serve Him. They are his army. He works to bring a close cooperation between the angels and humanity, warning of impending disasters. His aim is to protect us and guide us so that we may remain on the path of Light. He stands behind us when we call on Him.

Astrologically, the autumn equinox occurs when the sun enters Libra, the sign of the scales. It is a time for decision. The decision we must make is whether we want darkness or Light. It is a time when we must look at what we value and choose between the lower and higher qualities. Through Michael we are called to transmute qualities of the lower nature and asked to embody the higher quality of faith. We are asked to stand with Michael and defend the faith and to slay the dragon which tempts us to deny our true spiritual destiny and stay bound instead to the material nature.

The autumn equinox is also a time of judgement where our karma is considered and bestowed upon us for the coming year. According to Heline:[18]

The autumn equinox is a time for reaping the karmic fruits of past sowing and a time for sowing the spiritual seeds that will come to fruition when the same point is reached in the next annual cycle.

It is also a time when we may see a blueprint of the Plan. We see what is to come and what we must do to achieve that aim. At the autumn equinox perhaps more than any other time in the year we become aware of our free will and the choice that we must make if we are to take responsibility for our spiritual path. We are free to choose - Light or dark. Michael stands as an example of the choice for Light and shows us time and time again that he stands victorious as the dragon slayer. By aligning with Him, and calling Him to our aid we, too, can stand victorious in Light and not fall into the pits of darkness that lay before us. At this time we take the essence of the previous year's learning and find within it, through transmutation, the wisdom of lessons learned which can guide us to do better in the future. We are shown what we need to do to redeem ourselves and we are given opportunity to remain faithful to that task. It is a time when we are called to acknowledge and redeem the shadow aspects of ourselves. We are asked to deal with the shadow effectively that we may find harmony and move beyond the opposites that are contained within ourselves. It is a time of testing where we are to balance our karma with our deeds and stand before the Christ who is the judge, knowing that where we have been sincere, we will be met with divine mercy and love. If we are able to rise to the challenge, and if we have sowed well in the previous year, we will reap the karma. Yet the disciple needs also to be prepared at this time to surrender even that reaping. Whatever may be the disciple's yearning, the disciple surrenders to "Not my but Thy will be done." By surrendering and making sacrifice the disciple is purified and the needed transmutation is complete. By visualising Michael and asking to be one with the Christ Light we are lifted in consciousness and we become Light. As we do this we assist Michael in the spiritualisation of humanity and the planet. We assist in the unfoldment of the Plan which is essentially to spiritualise all life on the planet. We become more free as we pass through the gate and begin to sense the liberation that comes from transmutation and transformation. We are freed to be able to again serve in clarity and lightness.

Michael guides the evolution of Earth and humanity. He also assists us in overcoming domination by the negative forces. He has helped to reveal the mystery of the Christ. According to Heline, Archangel Michael, together with the other three main Archangels Gabriel, Raphael and Uriel, was present at the Holy Birth of the Lord Jesus. He was present at Gethsemane and foretold of the Resurrection and the Ascension. Heline also states that He was the guardian of the sixth century B.C. - the golden age of antiquity. This was the time of Buddha, Lao Tse, Confucius and Pythagoras. At this time, Michael supervises celestial operations on Earth.

Heline[19] states

> *Michael's most important work is the Christing of men's minds; that is, the preparing of human thought as a seed-ground for the implantation of the Christ awareness. Any individual thus illumined will think only Christed thoughts, speak only Christed words and perform only Christed deeds ... Part of Michael's mission is to spiritualise science ... resulting in a gradual emergence of a science of the soul.*

Michael stands for truth and calls upon us to spiritualise ourselves and in so doing become Christed.

The Lord Archangel Michael overshadowed King Arthur. The Excalibur sword is a symbol of His presence. With Michael behind him, King Arthur and his Knights of the Round Table could embody the qualities of all that is good in their rulership. When Arthur was without the sword, and symbolically without Michael, he lost his power. Through this legend it was shown that to have Michael behind you and thus have the power of the sword one has to be pure of heart.

It was Archangel Michael who overshadowed Joan of Arc. She, too, carried a special sword which gave her both the power to act and protection. She told of her Divine guidance and was loyal to her guiding angel even with the threat of and the actual event of her death.

The music associated with Michael is powerful deva music. A good example of this music is Sibelius' first symphony.

ARCHANGEL GABRIEL

Christmas time, the northern hemisphere's winter solstice and the southern hemisphere's summer solstice, is the time when Gabriel begins his reign. The Christ Light reaches the inner centre of the globe and remains there for four days. The sphere of the Earth is impregnated with the Christ's Light. The birth of the son brings a new growth cycle. The Earth and all life on it experience a fresh beginning. Each year this beginning is on a higher level of the evolutionary spiral. The Christ impulse emanates, energising and regenerating Spirit so that planetary conditions grow more favourable to humanity's spiritual awakening and fulfilment.

The northern winter solstice relates Holy Birth. It is the time when the Christ is born within our hearts. As Jesus went through his process in his mission, so we go through this same process of having the birth of Christ in our hearts. Every year the Christ comes to Earth as its redeemer, re-enacting on a cosmic scale the birth of the Risen Christ. At each winter solstice the Christ is born again. This spiritual impulse strengthens the love principle in the heart of humanity. Christmas is a redemptive period. Whether we are conscious of it or not, we all are exposed to the Divine radiation working redemptively in our earthly sphere. When individuals participate in this activity with understanding and spiritual intent, their inner enrichment is increased enormously. The Christ has made the Mysteries available to every seeking soul. We all have the opportunity to go through what Christ went through on the inner. Perhaps not in as majestic a way, but in our own ways, according to our own development.

At the northern winter solstice, the Christ Light enfolds the Earth. Earth experiences the inflow of Divine Light. According to Heline, the forces of the Cosmic Christ are concentrated in the heart of the planet in the form of a glorious mystic star. Its influence permeates the globe, transforming it into a mass of golden light on all levels of existence. The rite of the winter solstice purifies the planet itself. Even the mineral kingdom is touched by the Light. This spiritualisation of matter is accomplished largely by means of sound. The Christ gives the keynote. Humanity, through the help of the Avatars and messengers of Light, may become privy to the incoming messages and energies of transformation. These have great effect, even though they cannot be understood by the minds of humanity. This sound and energy we have come to know as 'The Living Word.'

The period of Gabriel's reign is when the sun is in Capricorn, Aquarius and Pisces. It is during these energies that the redemption of the dragon takes place. Through this period, the darkness is gathered up and destroyed. To understand this it is important to understand something of Gabriel's message of love. Archangel Gabriel is the messenger of universal and unconditional love. At Christmas time, the gates of initiation open and we are given the opportunity to receive the Light that is appropriate for us at that time. All living matter absorbs this Light according to its capacity to receive, so we as human beings on that eve and during that period of the solstice are able to take in the Light according to our capacities to receive.

> *The Disciple who observes from the Door of the Temple, must learn to focus his attention so one-pointedly in the idea of cosmic life that there can be no negative reaction; then the atoms of his body respond to the immortality-giving vibrations of the Christ Song as it emanates from the heart of the Earth and from the Sun.* (Heline[20])

Christmas time is a time of forgiveness. It is a time when people come together and let go of what they hold against each other, finding in their hearts true forgiveness for all brothers and sisters. We cannot enter into the gates of initiation holding grievances that we may have against each other. To enter we must redeem the dragon within us, and in so doing transform our darkness. This is part of the message of Gabriel. He brings the message of all-embracing love.

As mentioned earlier, Gabriel had a major role as teacher and counsellor to Lady Mary, in the mission of Jesus and the Path of love and service. It is for this guiding presence that Archangel Gabriel has become quite well known. The bringing of this exalted mystery to humanity has been his main mission. Through it he assisted Mary to became the way-shower, as He is to souls everywhere.

Gabriel's role of messenger can be seen throughout history where he has brought tidings of joy and warnings of disaster. (See previous notes on Archangel Gabriel under Ray 4.) It is interesting that this messenger role is also the role of Lady Mary at this time and during the early nineteenth century in France, at Lourdes, where Mary was seen to be warning humanity. She tells humanity that we need to change our ways in order for the Christ Light to be able to help us.

Gabriel's main colour is blue. For Gabriel, the main piece of music is "Ave Maria" by Schubert and Bach-Gonoud. It is because of his major role in assisting Mary in her work with Master Jesus that this song is a salute and tribute to His work and to the Love and Light of Lady Mary. In some versions of the pieces, the Schubert piece is sung by a female singer with a backing choir and the Bach-Gonoud piece is sometimes sung by a small boy.

As we said earlier, the emblem of Gabriel is the lily which is also the symbol of the Immaculate Conception. The lily is the symbol of purity. When purity and self-control have been achieved, a new organ develops within the etheric body of the head. This new organ emits a Light that has the outline of a lily blossom. It extends from the larynx upward.

> *It is this etheric organ, connecting the larynx with the spiritual organs within the head, which enables the Adept to speak the creative word and to take part in the Earth Ceremonial of the Christ Mass. All nine of the Lesser Initiations are required to bring this holy plant to its full flowering.* (Heline[21])

The esoteric understanding of Christmas strengthens the Love Principle. The celebrations at the Holy Night are evidenced also in earlier civilisations. In Egypt the winter solstice was celebrated with ceremonies paying homage to the divine Mother Isis and her new-born son Horus. It is also at this time that other great Avatars have been known to receive their illuminations and through that power, heal the Earth and humanity.

On the Holy Night the Temple doors open and the aspirant who is deemed worthy and qualified to experience the Christ Birth within, if the preparatory work has been well done, may begin a new life.

It is at this time we come to realise when we've been holding things against other people, and come to realise where we have made errors, where we have not lived according to even our own ideals. It is also at this time that Gabriel's message of love is very strong on many levels.

The following instance that occurred between two men is an illustration of the kind of alchemy and transmutation that takes place within us at Christmas time, when we realise things that we have done wrong. This story also tells of the way in which Archangel Gabriel is working against separatism and towards unity regardless of race, creed or colour. We can learn to love, even our enemies.

They had been friends since boyhood and in their early years they dreamed together and planned on spending their lives in joint enterprises. But as they grew older their religious beliefs divided them, one being a Catholic and the other a Protestant. They concluded that it would be wiser for each to go his own way, though the separation would bring deep hurt to them both; for theirs was a bond like unto that of David and Jonathan and could not be lightly cut asunder. Both men were successful and both attained to positions of eminence in the world of affairs. Passing from this Earth life only a few weeks apart, they presently found each other in their bodies of light. With the arrival of the holy Christmas Season they were drawn together to study etheric records wherein they looked back upon their Earth lives with an understanding not previously within their grasp. They now saw how narrow creedal beliefs had dimmed their understanding and how groundless were their reasons for separation. In the light of the great eternal verities, it became clear that what really counts is the kind of life one lives, not the theological doctrines one follows or the religious organisation to which one belongs. As this joyous realisation was borne in upon them they once again clasped hands. Soul met soul in a wordless communion which transcended human speech and carried the assurance that never again need there be parting. (Heline[22])

This very beautiful piece shows what we need to learn. It shows the need to look beyond our cultures and belief systems to the heart of those who are around us. We need to remind ourselves of our ideals and try to live according to them.

Gabriel works on the fourth Ray of purity, beauty, balance and harmony, with the Lord Serapis Bay. Gabriel means 'Hero of God'. He is aware of the Divine Plan of each life stream and he holds the Divine Concept for individuals in humanity and the Earth.

Lady Hope, as mentioned, is the twin ray of Archangel Gabriel. Where Archangel Gabriel is working for Love, to help us move beyond separatism to a place of higher celestial love, the Archangel Hope is working to instil and sustain hope and enthusiasm in everyone. This quality of hope is found in the Spirit of Resurrection. The Spirit of Resurrection is an energy emitted from the Great Cosmic Being Who is the Spirit of Resurrection. It contains the Holy Spirit with much heart and a transformative quality that assists us in our evolution. When we make errors it is easy to sit in a state of hopelessness and despair, not to forgive ourselves and hence not to continue working for the Light. The Lady Hope comes to remind us we must go on, and not rest in defeat. Hope lives deep within us. Lady Hope works in the temple of Resurrection with Gabriel and Raphael, giving the feeling of expectancy and upliftment. On days when we feel depressed, we can call on Lady Hope to intensify the energy of hope in our heart centres. She will help us to redeem the dragon inside, the negative aspect of ourselves, the shadow. It is through hope that we can overcome our darkness. Hope is one of the first steps on the path. When we embrace it, we open once more to the energy of love.

In Aikido training, falling is not seen as defeat. It is seen as a way to naturally protect ourselves, as a time and space in which we go within to regain ground. If one is concerned about how one looks when one is falling, the fall does not protect us, it hurts, it does not help us regain ground. For the fall to be beneficial, and give the needed momentum to rise easily again, there needs to be an acceptance and trust, and a preparedness to go with the flow of Spirit. This training forms an analogy to our spiritual growth. As we walk the Path, in the process of our growth we sometimes err. There is something we need to learn. When we err we may feel that we somehow 'fall' from grace, or as though we are falling or are about to fall off the Path. This may be so, yet it is often as we fall that we are tested still - to see how we will respond. Will we go into guilt and hopelessness, and remain inert, motionless, and begin to be usurped by the fear of making mistakes? Or will we face our error, realise our shortcomings, see what is needed to be learned, take it in, learn it and move on?

If we call on the quality of Hope, especially in such times as these, we find that instead of falling prey to hopelessness and despair and failing yet another test, we can rise to a place where we can see the learning needed, and we can find forgiveness for ourselves and others. We are given courage to dare to see the truth of ourselves, and we find faith that there is yet life and Light at the end of the tunnel.

Hope also helps us open to the needed qualities of love and joy. We are by hope transformed and awakened to our Christ-selves once again. We discover what is the Will of God. In times of darkness hope comes as a light for which we have yearned, like water to an unquenched thirst in a desert. It makes us fertile again, not barren and empty - and we remember - we have come to serve. Let us now call on the Lady Hope to work with us and let us awaken to the truth of ourselves, that we may enter into the love of the Christ and yearn only to serve Him. Let us open to the joy of service as the Archangels do.

ARCHANGEL RAPHAEL

Raphael becomes guardian of the spiritual evolution of humanity at the gate of Aries. He oversees the Easter Festival. Two symbols are associated with Him. They are the Holy Grail, which became his symbol after the occurrence of the Christ Mysteries, and the caduceus, or staff of Mercury, a staff entwined by two serpents, one white, the other black. Raphael is said to come from Mercury, and is said to have been closely connected with Hermes, the God of healing, who trained under Aesculapius, the great healer who was the son of Apollo and who was able to raise the dead[23]. Raphael is the Archangel of healing. He sends comfort and mercy to those in need. It is no accident that He comes on the fifth Ray, the Ray of Knowledge, for He knows exactly what is needed in order for healing to take place. He knows the remedy, the ingredients required for healing. Like the other Archangels, He has legions of angels at his command who work with Him, bringing comfort and mercy to those in need. In Hebrew legend Raphael is often spoken of in terms of healing. Many paintings of Him see Him depicted with Tobias.

This story of Tobias is written of in the Book of Tobit. Raphael instructs Tobias what he must do to heal his father's blindness and his bride-to-be's madness Heline[24] tells us:

> *There is a lovely legend to the effect that each eventide Raphael gathers up all prayers for healing which have arisen from mankind during the day and carries them up into heaven, where as he presents them before the Throne of God they are transformed into fragrant blossoms, which are then borne down to Earth by his serving angels to bring solace and comfort wherever there is pain and sorrow.*

Raphael's healing powers are sometimes evidenced in pictures where small wings are drawn at the throat indicating that the Word of Christ is spoken. This may happen in certain initiates who have the Christ in the mind and heart. Raphael also plays a major part in the Winged Healing Impulse which is helping humanity rise from the denseness of its matter to become half-human and half-angelic. The Winged Healer

Impulse is a special blend of the Christ Light and the Spirit of Resurrection which makes the merging of the human-self with the angelic-self possible.

Raphael is the Archangel of Resurrection. At Easter we experience world-wide resurrection and ascension where a new humanity will come to understand the truth of immortality and the triumph of Spirit over matter. Easter is the season of transmutation, transformation and transfiguration. Where we have become spiritually dead we are asked to rise from the tomb. The dross of our old nature is burned away under the fiery impulse of Aries. We are then released into a new and inspiring life.

The corresponding events in the life of Jesus Christ is the Last Supper and the burial in the tomb preceding the resurrection and the events of Golgotha.

> *On Golgotha, the Christ took upon Himself the burden of this world, and so lifted the mass consciousness of the race to make initiation possible to all.* (Heline[25])

Traditionally in Greek and Christian lore, Good Friday is often experienced as a time of great sorrow. It is, however, a time for celebration. It is a celebration because there is opportunity for transmutation and transformation. The disciple has opportunity for rebirth, and has come to a point of "Not my but Thy will be done." There is opportunity for resurrection, to lift ourselves and our lives to a higher place. Easter is also a time of celebration as it represents the re-enactment of the Christ's Resurrection and we can re-experience how the Christ Light is able to come to us on Earth through that process of death, resurrection and ascension. The death we must endure is an inner one.

At Easter many spiritual organisations celebrate with an Easter temple ceremony. This is overseen by Archangel Raphael. For many, this time marks a time of initiation depending on the effort made by the aspirant or disciple in the time preceding the Festival. At this time the power of the Christ Spirit is evidenced at the full moon. In the Easter ceremony, the Lord Christ is accompanied by many angelic beings. Music such as "Gloria in Excelsis Deo" calls to the angels. Music of an infinite nature such as Wagner's "Parcifal" and "Lohengrin" may be used as a symbol of our quest for the Grail (the Christ Spirit) and the quest for the eternal Light. Mahler's "Resurrection" also brings forth the attention of the angels and lifts us to their heights. Raphael comes as the angel of immortality healing us through death to new life.

ARCHANGEL URIEL

Archangel Uriel comes into His reign at the time of the northern hemisphere's summer solstice at the gate of Cancer. When the sun is in Cancer, the Christ fashions the matrix of his body of Light. In the middle of his reign, the matrix is infused with the power of love. This is at the time of the sign of Leo which rules the heart. In the last part of his reign when the sun is in Virgo, the Christ Ray touches the Earth's atmosphere and the planetary conception is complete.

The summer solstice, winter time in the southern hemisphere, is a period of transformation and ascension. It is the esoteric Christian Festival of the Ascension of the Christ.
At the solstices the streams of life force pour down upon the Earth. These Rays are disseminated to us, some through the Christ, some through the Archangel Uriel and some through Archangel Gabriel

The summer solstice is a time when the Christ is going through his own process of ascension when he is lifted up to the throne of God. The energies are very strong and they have to be transformed down to us on Earth while that process takes place. Rays are received and disseminated by the Christ and are sent to those who are found worthy of initiation. Light is given to those who are ready for creative and artistic inspiration. It also goes to the mass of humanity. We can have people all seated in one room, all of different degrees and levels of initiation, and the Light will give to each what that person is ready for and able to receive. In very powerful energies, some can be initiated, while others are being inspired, and still others are simply lifted by the Light. At midnight the door of the temple opens to those who are worthy and the cosmic Christ is reborn into the Christed consciousness, entering into unity with life eternal.

We have seen here that one of Uriel's tasks is to inspire creativity in us. He is working on the sixth Ray, the Ray of Devotion. It is often through devotion that we are inspired to do our works. Devotion inspires people to create. He works very closely with Master Jesus and Lady Nada. He is the interpreter of the prophecies, the Angel of retribution and salvation. His name means Light of God. He heals the Earth and dispenses spiritual Light. According to Heline, beauty and vision are his key notes. He helps us to slowly open our inner vision.

Many who are sensitive to inner-plane conditions are able at this time to contact angelic beings more easily and more intimately than at any other time of the year. The festivals of Pentecost and Asala, which precede the summer solstice by only a short time, have filled the disciples, aspirants and humanity with the Holy Spirit Light, sending the Spirit of Resurrection to the dove- and lion-hearted ones. The following solstice, which takes place sometimes only eight to ten days later, is a time when, with the Christ Light in us, we can open more intimately to the angelic beings and work with them. Early alchemists and esotericists learnt to take full advantage of the uplifting energies of this time for bringing the great Plan to perfection. Spiritual activity at this time works towards purification and sanctification of the Earth and humanity. People are inspired to be of service in a warm, kind and joyful way.

The play "A Midsummer Night's Dream," written by Shakespeare, was an inspired work of art that represents the inner world movement at this time. It has opened the portals of the fairy world to humanity. In the play, Shakespeare describes the angelic kingdom's work with nature, conveying the true splendour of Light and colour.

As said earlier, during this time of Uriel's reign, at the summer solstice, the Sermon on the Mount was given. People even today are asked to learn to apply the transcended truth of this sermon in daily life.

The following quotes come from that sermon.

> *Seeing the crowds he went up on the mountain, and when he sat down his disciples came to him, and he opened his mouth and taught them saying, "Blessed are the poor in spirit for theirs is the kingdom of heaven, blessed are those who mourn for they shall be comforted, blessed are*

the meek for they shall inherit the Earth, blessed are those who hunger and thirst for righteousness for they shall be satisfied, blessed are the merciful for they shall obtain mercy, blessed are the pure in heart for they shall see God, blessed are the peace makers for they shall be called sons of God, blessed are those who are persecuted for righteousness sake for theirs is the kingdom of heaven, blessed are you when men revile you and persecute you and utter all kinds of evil against you falsely, on my account rejoice and be glad for your reward is great in heaven, for so men persecuted the prophets who were before you, you are the salt of the Earth, but if salt has lost its taste how shall its saltiness be stored? It is no longer good for anything except to be thrown out and trodden under foot by men. You are the Light of the world, a city set on a hill cannot be hid, nor do men light a lamp and put it under a bushel but on a stand and it gives light to all in the house. Let your light so shine before men that they may see your good works and give glory to your father who is in heaven. Think not that I have come to abolish the law and the prophets, I have come not to abolish them but to fulfil them, for truly I say to you till heaven and Earth pass away not an iota, not a dot will pass from the Law until all is accomplished. Who ever then

*relaxes one of the least of these commandments
and teaches men so shall be called least in the
kingdom of heaven but he who does them and
teaches them shall be called great in the kingdom
of heaven for I tell you unless your righteousness
exceeds that of the scribes and Pharoasees you
will never enter the kingdom of heaven.*

*You have heard that it was said an eye for an
eye, and tooth for a tooth but I say to you, do
not resist one who is evil but if anyone strikes
you on the right cheek turn to him the other
also and if anyone would sue you and take your
coat, let him have your cloak as well. And if
anyone forces you to go one mile, go with him
two miles. Give to him who begs from you and
do not refuse him who would borrow from you.
You have heard that it was said you shall love
your neighbour and hate your enemy but I say
to you love your enemies, and pray for those who
persecute you so that you may be sons of your
father who is in heaven, for he makes his son
rise on the evil and on the good and sends rain
on the just and on the unjust, for if you love
those who love you what reward have you? Do
not even the tax collectors do the same and if
you salute only your brethren what more are you
doing that others? Do not even the gentiles do*

the same? You therefore must be perfect as your heavenly father is perfect. When you pray you must not be like the hypocrites for they love to stand and pray in synagogues and at the street corners that they may be seen by men. Truly I say to you they have received their reward but when you pray, go into your room and shut the door and pray to your father who is in secret and your father who sees in secret will reward you. And in praying do not heap up empty phrases for they might think that they will be heard for their many words. Do not be like the gentiles for your father knows what you need before you ask him.' And then he gave the world prayer, 'Our Father who art in heaven, hallowed be thy name, thy kingdom come, thy will be done as Earth as it is in heaven, give us this day our daily bread and forgive us our debts, as we also have forgiven our debtors, and lead us not into temptation but deliver us from evil. For if you forgive men their trespasses your heavenly father will also forgive you but if you do not forgive men their trespasses neither will your father forgive your trespasses. Blessed are the peacemakers for they shall inherit the Earth (The New Testament[26], Matthew 5-7).

These great words of wisdom stand still able to teach us today. Such Divine inspiration, spoken through the great Avatar

Jesus, as well as we are able to have recorded Him, gives some insight into Uriel's role of opening our vision and helping us to interpret the prophecies.

Uriel works very much in the Earth's atmosphere, penetrating the core of the Earth with the Christ Light. Through him physical activities are made complete. Like Raphael, he acts on people's prayers.

We have considered the work of all the Archangels and begin to see how each plays His or Her own unique part in the Plan. Yet the cooperation between them and the intertwining nature of their tasks reveal the intricate and powerful nature of their work in assisting the spiritual development of the Earth and humanity. By looking more closely at the work of the four main Archangels we have seen how the seasons symbolise the Path of Initiation, leading through Birth, Crucifixion, Resurrection and Ascension. During the equinoxes and solstices, in all seasons, the Masters of Wisdom give the needed spiritual teachings to the world, and assist us along on the Path of spiritual evolution.

TARAJYOTI   GOVINDA

the ANGELIC HELPERS

THE ANGELIC HELPERS

The angels' wings are the healing hands of love. The angels teach us how to heal, and to those who are open to them, they become constant companions in life, always helping to lift and make light of our troubles and burdens, guiding and guarding the way. Angels are our mentors, teachers, and friends in Spirit, who help us to unite with Spirit and find unity and oneness in our hearts and minds. In this chapter we will look at the angelic kingdom and try to understand something of the angels' inner nature.

The angels come to us as messengers of God. We are blessed with angelic guidance and with guardians who seek to assist us in our spiritual development. The angels may warn us when there is disaster, and assist us in our process of birth and death, in our daily life on Earth, and in the after-life, where some of us walking the Earth now may then function in the angelic form. Many people are not conscious of the love and assistance the angels give them. Yet for many the veil is being lifted and the help and vision of the angels are becoming evident. More of humanity is being awakened to the beauty of a life lived in conscious awareness of angelic help and the cherished companionship they give. Once we discover this contact, we know deep in our hearts that we are never alone.

We must ask for help to be given help. That is the Law. I have been working as a spiritual healer for many years. In that time I have not ceased to be amazed at the wondrous efforts of the angels. They bring insight, revelation, faith, hope and forgiveness to many a needy heart. They help us to lift out of our more negative nature and see the world in a new Light, bringing vision and trust, restoring us to a state where we can reconnect with God within.

The angels live on the inner levels and work with colour, Light and symbol. They communicate through the language of the heart, expounding the virtues of goodness and all that is holy. In their Light we are lifted to the Love of God, and experience the sense of unity that brings. We can ask the angels to help lift us to their special vibration where they can communicate with us. When we are down, we can ask for their help to lift us and they will give it readily. In their Light we may receive messages of a joy and peace we never dreamed possible. Let us open to the angels and their special message. Open now to their message for you.

THE FORM OF THE ANGELS

The angels have no physical body as humans do. They have a body of Light which enables them to move and function swiftly in the world of Light. They are normally unseen by the human eye; however, when the veil is lifted and clairvoyant or clairsentient faculties are used, they can be seen and felt. The angels are on a path of evolution, as we are. They are working towards unity with the Divine as we walk towards unity on the Path to Perfection.

We are both children of Father-Mother God. The angels live to serve the unfoldment of the Plan, while we in our denser matter strive to consciously cooperate with the Plan, and aspire to serving in a similar manner. When we look through our inner eyes, the angels become visible to us. The air about us is full of them. They live in Nature, wherever there is Divine life. They evolve through their inner work. Some dwell in crystals, in the woods and gardens, some are attracted to the elements of water, fire, air or earth. There are angels who have the task of assisting human beings in their evolution, and guardian angels who are angels protecting us as we walk the spiritual path. It is our guardian angels who help us to align to the will of the soul. The guardian angels are the angels who guide us and are our guardians helping us to lift our consciousness and vibration to that of Light.

Angels move so freely in the world of Light, flying with the speed of Light. They do not have feathers as they are sometimes depicted as having. Their wings are a concentrated mass of Light that is part of their bodily existence, and which, when we look through the inner eye, may appear like wings. Their inner form is radiant, colourful and made of particles of Light. Through their Light and their colour, they communicate with us, making symbols through which we can discern and comprehend their message. The colour may vary; for example, when looking at the army of winged healing Light beings assisting the Archangel Raphael, the wings at first appear to be a deep emerald green. On looking more closely at the concentration of Light evident in the wings, the richest violet can be seen, depicting not only their healing nature, but their ability to transform all that they touch. We may say that they are so richly emerald green they are violet. To find something to illustrate this on the physical plane, perhaps we could liken it to the richness of the colours of the feathers of a peacock, which have a luminous quality and profound depth and beauty.

The people in the East have often called angels "devas" which means "the shining ones." Angels have a very dynamic energy and a vividness of consciousness and of life. It is said that angels may even guide the artists into drawing the angels as they are. Sometimes the faces may appear human but on a closer look they are not; sometimes the eyes may be full of Light. Such Light is rarely seen amongst human beings.

HOW CAN WE RECOGNISE THEM?

When angels come, people often feel the love and the sense of self-acceptance and inner peace that is given, and feel recognised and deeply cared for. They may simply have a tingling in their hearts, and they will feel themselves becoming more open-hearted than is their normal state of being. Of course, the physical signs sometimes come, such as goose bumps, tingling at the back of the neck, tears, heightened clarity of vision or a beautiful fragrant smell.

In the theosophical view, the Archangels are the head of the angelic kingdom. Christianity also speaks of the ranks of angels: Thrones, Dominions or Dominations, Principalities, Virtues, Powers, Cherubim, and Seraphim. According to Geoffrey Hodson in *The Kingdom of the Gods*, to each of these types of angels certain qualities and activities are assigned. "Archangels are sent as messengers in matters of high importance," as we have seen through Gabriel, Raphael, Michael and Uriel. "The Cherubim excel in the splendour of knowledge;" Seraphim "inspire with Divine Love;" and the Thrones are known for the "glory and equity of the divine judgements." The Cherubim enlighten through wisdom; the Seraphim motivate with love; the Thrones teach us to use our discrimination and judgement. Dominions "regulate the activities and duties of the angels," and the "Principalities preside over people and Provinces and serve as angelic rulers of nations of the world." Devas of particular countries, national devas we call them, come into this last category. "Powers keep a check on negative energies. Virtues have the gift of working miracles".[27]

Hodson[28] describes the angelic kingdom in terms of the greater and the lesser Gods. The greater Gods to which Hodson refers are the angels and the Archangels. He talks of the lesser Gods as being the smaller nature spirits which take both astral and etheric forms. The gnomes, fairies, brownies, elves and tree manikins come to life in his descriptions of them, made more vivid by our memory of "fairytales" from childhood. It is most heartening to read about how these beings mimic human form and dress, and awaken a sense of play within us. Clairvoyant people bear witness to their existence and their descriptions match from all corners of the globe. Hodson talks of the landscape angels and spirits of the waterfalls called "undines," lake spirits, grass elves, dancing fairies and the fairy queen. We are here reminded of Shakespeare's *Midsummer Night's Dream*. Hodson also talks of the air spirits - sylphs, and fire spirits - salamanders which have relatively no fixed form. If one goes into nature it is possible to become aware of these small beings. Even if we cannot see them we can know of their existence and communicate with them. They make nature come alive for us. They help to mend our etheric bodies, and fill us with etheric energy when we go into nature - perhaps at the sea or the forest. Hence when we visit nature we return rejuvenated and often restored to good health.

THE NATURE OF THE ANGELS

The angels are by their nature tuned in to the Creative Intelligence, and love to create in a light and heartfelt manner. They are Light and their nature is Light. We may call it light-hearted. The ability they have to be joyful and bring humour can help to lighten up what might seem like the darkest of situations. They remind us not to be so serious in our quest, but instead to allow the universal forces to assist us to go through life in rhythm with the universal flow. Their symbolic language, when understood, provides insight from a high intelligence. They have a sharp mind and wit which help us to perceive their higher meaning.

The angels look from above and have the objectivity that we in our subjective feeling and thinking states lack. It makes sense, therefore, that if we truly wish to rise into the lightness of their vibration, we should call on them for help. They can lift us, they know our weak spots and are aware of our virtues, helping us to strengthen them, so that we can cooperate in the work for the Light.

CONTACTING THE ANGELS

To talk to the angels, we simply need to come to an open-hearted space. This may not sound so easy to some who have difficulty contacting their heart and to others who are hampered from contacting the angels through their negative inner voice. The angels do not resonate in unison with the negative ego which expresses itself through harsh self-criticism or blown up feelings of self-importance. If we feel that we have become arrogant, we can ask the angels to help us find humility again. If we feel we have become too self-denigrating, we can ask the angels to help us to find self-acceptance. When we go into negative mind and feeling states, we have to learn to be able to release the negativity instead of holding onto it. If we have difficulty letting go, we can call on the Angel of Release, who is an angel who helps us to let go of what we need to. I often think of it like this: if we fill our minds with worry about what may or may not happen in the future, or about what did or didn't happen in our past, no space is left in us to experience the present now. Similarly, if we hold on to grievances against others, our fear, our guilt, and our pain, no room is left to experience the joy, peace and love.

Worry and stress make it difficult for angels to contact us. Our astral bodies bloat up and our inner senses are thwarted. By maintaining calm and working at keeping our thoughts and feelings in balance and harmony through meditation, contemplation and healing, or simply by using positive thinking in our daily lives, we make it easier for the angels to connect with us. So the message is, lighten up and you too may be able to fly!!

LISTENING TO THE ANGELS AND OPENING TO CONTACT

If we want to hear the angels we need to stop and listen. This is also something that many of us are not good at. It can be learned and must be practiced. Be still and listen to the silent voice within. The throat chakra is the chakra connected with clairaudience and is our energetic centre of communication. If we wish to hear on the inner, we can still ourselves and listen to the silent voice. It may be heard from the heart centre, or we may sense it around the throat centre. It is audible not with our ears but from between them. We can affirm mentally, "I open my inner ear and my inner eye." This enables the angels to contact us in whatever way is most suitable. We become a receptive vehicle through this affirmation. Sometimes people align to the angels by feeling an expansion within the inner bodies and by coming into a deep resonance with the silence in which the angels speak.

To stimulate our throat centre, inner ear and inner eye we can use a song or chant that will help us align, provided we do it through our heart. The act of singing helps connect the heart and throat centres. We can even practice making vocal sounds until our body hums with their different tones. If we practise such exercises for the purpose of communicating with our angels, our angels will know it and will assist us to help find the answers we need.

Every effort we make to contact them will be met with enthusiastic response by them, as that is their nature. The intent alone is enough to initiate communication. When we communicate with our angels, it is as though our senses have heightened and we will be aware of moving to different levels of receptivity. The physical world may appear different when we return to it. Colours, shapes and sounds are heightened, or perhaps everything will appear less distinct. This awakens us to the knowing that there has been a shift in our vibration, and we are changed from the communion.

CREATING A DIALOGUE WITH THE ANGELS

When your angels come, you can talk to them as you could to another human being who you are beginning to know. They are different from human beings in the sense that they have great wisdom and know all there is to know about your path in life. You can ask them their names; you can ask them to help you find your purpose with questions like, "What is it I need to know now?" "How can I best serve?" It can be useful when interacting in this way to either have another person write down the information you receive or to have a pen and paper yourself where you can write it down. This helps you remember when you return to your usual state of consciousness. If your angel says its name is Raphael, Michael or Gabriel, it does not mean you are communicating with the

Archangels; however, it may mean that the angel comes from Gabriel's group or Michael's army.

You may even wish to have a tape-recorder nearby where you can speak and record the messages, or you may sit at your computer and type what you hear. The deep connection that comes with the angelic being can provide a great source of comfort and of pleasure. It can also bring illumination when you connect. The connection may come in a quiet moment. When you become aware of your breath and your body, the sounds of the outer world and the roles you play in it are minimised. You are given time out for a moment, to connect to the higher life, gaining insight and objectivity that has a sacred space, the space where God can be found.

As you practice, the communication can be lengthened, trust grows, and you are receptive to more help. The practice helps you let go of the need to be right and helps you know that there is a realm where more is known than you know. When you acknowledge that you need to learn more, you can, because you are open to it. When you think you know it all, you are incapable of learning more and the doors are closed to the higher knowledge.

ANGELS AND OUR CHILDHOODS

Many of us had imaginary friends as children and were in a lot of contact with the angelic kingdom. The angels love children as they are open and receptive, innocent and believing. They like to be called upon to guard over children and they respond easily to their playful natures. Many of the female Masters (Masters are great Beings who have walked the Lighted Path before us) such as Lady Nada, Lady Portia and Lady Yasodhara, and also the White Tara (who is a cosmic Being, an Avatar of Light) have angels assisting Them to bring the qualities of joy, compassion, acceptance, love and protection to children. By contacting our own inner child we too can become as receptive to the angels as children, letting angels in to help and guide us, making joyful and heartfelt connection.

Many children these days are more able to recognise the fairy or angel world. Often in the past, adults have taught children that this is not a real world. Perhaps now the adults can begin to learn from the children, to see and feel the angels in all their beauty and splendour.

THE ANGELS AND THEIR ROLE IN HEALING

Angels are on the path of evolution as we are, whereas elementals are on the path of involution or the downward path. If we wish to create a better atmosphere in our workplace, in our homes, and in our rooms, making our environment harmonious and pure, we can call upon the angels to drive away any negative influences. We need to use our own will and the help of the angels. They will help us charge the atmosphere with living Light and power. If we wish, we can ask them to stay and guard where we are cleansing, and maintain the purity and harmony which has been produced. If we could become aware of this ability that angels have, to help us purify not only our environment but also our minds and hearts from negative thoughts and feelings that often lead to negative actions, we could do a lot to help lift the consciousness of the Earth and many of the groups on it.

In *The Brotherhood of Angels and Men*, Geoffrey Hodson talks about the angels of power, the angels of the healing art, the guardian angels of the home, the angels of nature, music, beauty and art. He suggests we begin to cooperate with these angels to help with the unfoldment of God's Plan. To do this he suggests we develop purity, simplicity, directness and impersonality. Hodson also tells us, in his book *Angels and the New Race*, if we are to uplift the human race, we need to "bring the two branches of the infinite family of God into close cooperation."

As a way of invoking and calling upon the help of the angels, we can meditate in groups in a one-pointed and united effort. We can ask the angels to help with the special purpose we have in mind, provided it comes from a pure heart, a pure mind, and has good intent behind it. We can sit in the sacred symbol of the circle and direct our thoughts to the harmony and unity that we wish to create, until we feel ourselves become one with the angels. We can go to the inner planes to do the work, visualise it happening and visualise the angels at work. This helps us all to evolve.

Geoffrey Hodson in *Angels And The New Race*, gives this beautiful prayer:

> *Oh Holy Lord of Love, Teacher of angels and*
> *   of men,*
> *We invoke Thy mighty power in all its*
> *   splendour,*
> *Thy undying love in all its potency,*
> *Thy infinite wisdom in all its perfection,*
> *So that they may flow through us in a resistless*
> *   flood into this place or person.*
> *Before the living stream of Thy resistless power*
> *   all darkness shall melt away, the hearts of*

all men shall be changed, and they shall
seek and find the way of Light.

Amen.

Hodson tells us that after such a prayer, the silence and meditation which follows brings forth His glorious power. The group which is meditating can project the power of love with all the force and concentration of their united wills upon the place or person chosen as the recipient of their aid. The angels can be directed to act, to send the energy for the cause for which it was invoked. It is good to ask that the energy be sent to where it is needed most and leave where to the Lord of Love to decide.

The amount of love and peace and Light that is available is endless; it is an eternal well, available to those who have a pure heart. There is no limit to what this energy can do to help people who are suffering. If our hearts are open to the sufferings of people and we practice cooperating with each other and with the angelic kingdom, we will really increase our usefulness in the world.

To get to a point of being prepared and ready to do such work, we have to go through a purification process. In this individual healing process the angels can help us. We can call upon the angels of cleansing, the angels of purity, the angels of transmutation, the angels of courage and the angels of healing. We can also call upon the angels of the Christ to help quicken the process, provided we are ready, prepared and willing to do what needs to be done as a result. The evolution of the heart helps us to overcome the negative influences, and we can move towards helping the world become a Star of Light, which is its destiny.

The angels move quickly in the world of Light and are set in motion by the Will of God and the purified will of humanity. We can work to create a world which fulfils the purpose of our souls and one which brings forth the Light, Love and Plan of the Lord of Love, the Teacher of angels and humanity, the Christ. It is with the Lord of Love that God shall become known to all on Earth.

The angels, the shining ones, are experts at service. They can drive away suffering and depression, and can exorcise the powers of darkness and disease. If we work regularly with them, they become a reality to us, and when we call on them, they come. With their help we can become radiating centres of Light and open to spiritual life. When our motives are purified, when we will to serve, and when from our hearts we want to bring forth the Will of God into our lives and the lives of those around us, then we are ready to invoke the help of the angels. If we should try to use our will in a negative way, for example, with intent to harm others, or for purposes of selfish gain, then instead we create negativity and destroy any good work. We must learn to pray the ancient prayer, "Not mine but Thine Will be done."

When we call upon the angels, we can experience an increase in vitality beyond our normal capacity. Working in a way that is spiritual, mental and moral brings the angels to our aid. The angels inspire and strengthen our efforts. As we link ourselves with the power and presence of the inner worlds, we open to the guidance of the beings within it. We receive their help and their strength and are able to heal disease and relieve suffering. We move out of our ignorance about disease and suffering and recognise the reasons for it. We can help to dispel our ignorance by calling upon the angel of education, the angel of wisdom, the angel of love and the angel of higher understanding to help us.

If we really wish to help someone who is sick, it would be wise to call upon the angels, because they will bring the needed vitality to help the person become well, and will work in accordance with the karmic condition of that person. When a person has a karmic condition which may come as a disease, the angels can help by giving that person acceptance, peace of mind, a bright disposition, and the vitality he or she needs to do the tasks at hand. With pain or sickness, which is nature teaching us the Law, we can correct the errors of thought and action which have brought the suffering. We may even come to understand the reasons for our disease. We can pray to the Lord Christ, the great Healer and Counsellor of humanity with all of our heart and ask that He send His healing power to those suffering. The help may come on the inner rather than on the physical level, or it can come on both. It won't fail to come. We can mentally call upon the healing angels for their help, and ask them to be vehicles of the Christ Light and remain with the person until that person has returned to his or her health or wholeness, or has entered into his or her true dharma in life. This method is adopted by spiritual healers all over the planet and has been so for many ages. Only some recognise or acknowledge the presence and help of the angels in this work. When we consciously cooperate and acknowledge the Christ, there is an enormous increase in permanent result.

When people are depressed, we can ask the angels to lift the fog around them. We may try to invoke the person's good qualities. We can also, once we have done the healing work with the Christ Light, call upon the angels to rejuvenate and replenish the person's inner bodies with their radiant Light until the person is full of joy, Light and happiness. We can ask the angels to remain with our clients when we have finished our work, to help them in their daily lives until they have overcome the issue or problem. This is very often done with the angels of the pink Light. Lady Nada (one of the female Masters who works closely with the Lord Jesus) has millions of angels at her command. When we pray for healing, the angels are able to stay with the sick person and give him or her the courage and peace needed to get better.

THE ANGELS' ROLE IN THE PROCESS OF BIRTH

The nature spirits help to build our etheric bodies when we incarnate, the astral devas help to create our emotional body, and mental devas help to create our mental body. The angels help in the process of birth and in helping to create the astral, the etheric and the mental body of the incoming soul. An elemental works to create the etheric double, and the nature-spirits work with the etheric energy of the mother to create the etheric body. The astral angels work to create a safe environment for the mother and child during the pregnancy and birth, and to stop negative influences and harmful effects, according to the karma of the child. The mental angels have the knowledge of the karma of the individual, and within the aura of the mental angel the incoming soul's past lives can be seen. The nature spirits and angels work with and cooperate with the soul to help build the physical expression of the human being.

THE ANGELS' ROLE IN THE PROCESS OF DEATH

The angels play a major role in helping people in the transition from the earthly world to the inner worlds, and from the physical level to the etheric, astral and mental levels, depending upon what level they will reside on before they return to the next incarnation. Many people, as they approach death, become increasingly aware of the angelic helpers on the inner planes. Many relatives and friends of the dying who are left behind in grief are touched and moved by the awareness of comforting and support given to them from the angels. This is sometimes felt as a sense of knowing one is not alone. It can sometimes be felt like being gently touched, or words of comfort may be heard on the inner. Their help and comfort help to relieve and release the enormous pain of grief. Where necessary and where we have earned the karma for it, the angels can assist us to continue our work for the Light when we pass over.

THE MERGING

We are coming to a time when the blending of angelic and human life and consciousness is beginning to take place. This is part of the plan of the coming New Age. A very great flood of new life is coming upon the Earth through the Spirit of Resurrection. The Spirit of Resurrection is a great Light full of Holy Spirit and great heart. The Spirit of Resurrection is merging with the Light of Christ to bring forth the blending of angelic and human life and consciousness. As the Spirit of Resurrection sends its Light, a new form of human being comes forward in the form of the winged healer. Many of the old forms are swept away and new forms of beauty are coming. Humanity will have virtues that will make them more God-like; the principles of Right Human Relations will be lived. These are the principles of love and truth, justice and harmlessness.

THE GRACE OF COMING TO KNOW THE ANGELS

You may be aware that the angels are more closely connected with us now, because the veil between the inner and outer levels has lifted. There is a great deal of pain and suffering that humanity must yet go through. The grace has been given for the veil to be lifted so that we can become one with the angel kingdom and awaken our consciousness to that of the angels. It is time for us to wake up. As we have seen throughout history, angels come to warn of pending disaster, and they come now to do the same. It is time for us to listen, to wake up and change our ways, opening our hearts to love. Certain Masters and Archangels are working together with the Lord Christ, the Lord of Love, the Teacher of angels and humanity, to help us merge with the consciousness of the angels. When we do this, we become the new humanity, a group of people who will to live by the heart and prepare for the Lord of Love to come in about five hundred years. If we are to become the new humanity, we must open our hearts to our sisters and brothers in human and angelic form. The angels can help us clear the path and point out the way. It is for us to decide to fly with them, to open to the great love and peace they bring, and to remember that the love and peace they bring is the love and peace of the Christ, the Lord of Love.

METHODS OF DISCRIMINATING TRUE MESSAGES

How can you recognise a true angel? How do you know the messages you receive are of Light? If you are unaware about whether a message you have received is of Light, there are a number of things you can do to test it out.

Ask yourself,
>"Does this make sense?"
>"Is it helpful?"
>"Is it kind?"
>"Is it harmless?"

Use your imagination to consider what might happen if you implement the directions in your message. What are the gains? What are the losses? If you find the message given is helpful, you may wish to implement it. If you find it is decidedly unhelpful, you may discover that it is not, after all, of the Light. You may wish to meditate upon the message and see what that brings, or take it to a healing and contemplate it further before acting. If it is true, it will stand the test of time and will continue to reveal itself to you in a multitude of ways. It is important that you do not worry about it, for as you worry you stir up the clouds of astral matter and make it impossible for you to discriminate and discern what is true or not.

You must always remember to guard yourself against your own personality which has a tendency to conjure up a magic which is according to its own wishes. This does not mean that if an angel gives you a message and you are happy about it, you cannot trust it; it simply means you should proceed with caution and try to decide what is of your personality's making and what is the true message from the higher forces of Light. You cannot expect to be able to know immediately, for the process of discernment takes time and a concentrated method of analysis, with a view to being receptive of the truth.

We live in a world where we are accustomed to instant gratification and we must learn that things that last and are of value take time to build in energy. We need to train ourselves to be at peace in our process, regardless of outcome. In this way we learn the lesson of non-attachment, and we allow our lives to be guided by the higher forces of love and Light.

When people try to find inner contact, it is possible that they may make contact with their own astral body or their own mental body and feel that they have made contact with something higher, especially if the message from their astral body suits their personality wishes. Many who think they are in contact with higher beings are not, and many who do not presume to be, are.

FURTHER SIGNS OF TRUE ANGELS

If you really wish to discover the truth of whether you are in contact with angels or not, there are a few things you really need to understand. If you sincerely wish from your heart to contact an angel and you do not get a response straight away, you can rest assured that the angel will hear you. It doesn't matter whether you think you are in contact or not, you can talk to the angels. It is through the angel that God hears you. When you are in contact, it is likely that you will feel happy and uplifted and have a warm glow. Sometimes the hairs will stand up on end or there is a sudden rush of energy through the body, a tingling at the back of the neck or a funny feeling in the heart. Trust plays an important part in contacting the angels. A person healing with the help of the angels has to trust that the person has been healed. You must trust that you have been heard. The effects may not be immediate and may come later. You cannot let your expectations and demands interfere with the trust and knowing. You can't expect great clairvoyant phenomena; you must simply know that the angels do hear and act according to the Will of God. Your karma must also be considered. It may be that even several years later your answers will come, as God in His-Her infinite wisdom may need you to learn certain lessons first. You need to be ready to receive God's gifts. It may be also that you need to prove this to yourself. It is when you come to live as the angels do, to give without counting the cost, to give in return

TARAJYOTI GOVINDA

for the love and Light you receive that you can truly open to God's gift of Spirit.

If you are touched by the angels, you are touched by God and you will change your life. It is at such times as near-death experiences, when the angels come in close contact, that you see evidence of this. People report the blessing of the great Light and communication with angels at such times of crisis. When people have these experiences, their whole life changes and they need to put these changes into action. It is after the near-death experience that people seem suddenly to want to give and find themselves moving into fields of humanitarian work. Many books are appearing now which have researched and accounted for these changes in people resulting from near-death experiences.

The touch of the angels makes people believe in the existence of God. In near-death experiences and also when there is a trauma in life and the help of the angels is felt, a raising of consciousness occurs. It is as if the veil has been lifted. Seeing the glory of the inner worlds gives hope and faith before unknown. Such experiences are not something you forget; they can stay with you in this and many lives to come.

Powerful experiences such as these may be likened to the experience of those who have seen the eyes of Jesus: they will never forget this experience and the memory will assist them to work for the Christ, in this life and in those to come.

When people go through the near-death experience, they usually lose the fear of death because they realise how active they can become when the physical garment is cast away and they are free to move in the Light. In the inner worlds they can help so much, as they are free to move so quickly and assist those in need.

HOW CAN THE ANGELS HELP US?

Some angels know our karma and they are linked with the Grace of God. Sometimes the Grace is given and the karma released, sometimes the karma must be played out; but when we ask for the help of the angels, the help is given. Perhaps it will come in an understanding of our situation and our part in creating it; perhaps we will be spared going through something we feel we cannot face. The karma and the Grace can unfold in our lives in a multitude of ways, but when we pray to the angels we come to know that we are not alone during the unfolding. We can endure anything that is given to us to endure, for we come to understand its role in helping us to grow and helping us to come to accept God's plan. In so accepting we can become closer to God through the angels, and feel the blessing that this gives. No longer separate and alone, we are unified with the Divine even in our vulnerability, for it is our vulnerability that takes us to Him-Her. We must always remember that the angels are the Messengers of God and that they bring the Love, the Light and the Care of God with them, along with the great Wisdom and Heart of enormous intelligence and compassion.

In our little worlds it is difficult for us to comprehend the greatness of this Universe, yet we are a microcosm of it and can experience within ourselves the battle of Light and dark. By calling on the angels we strengthen the Light in us. We come to know the Christ-self and experience the birth of Christ within our hearts. The Lord Archangel Michael Who is the Defender of the Faith, the Protector of the Earth, is the Archangel Who brings forth God's Plan and gives us the blue-print of what is to come. He serves the Lord of Love, Who is the Unifier, the Teacher of angels and humanity. The Lord of Love, the Lord Maitreya, reveals to us the Plan for His coming in the next five hundred years. The angels work ceaselessly to assist in the unfoldment of the Plan through their understanding of the Hierarchy that exists within the angelic kingdom, where every being within that kingdom seeks to serve the Light, dedicated to its task. We are given a vision of how we could choose to cooperate and help the Earth reach its destiny as a Star of Light. To do this we must call upon the help of the angels. We must believe in them, for they can set us free and bring the liberation of Spirit that we need to release ourselves from the shackles of our unredeemed past. Then we can work and cooperate for the Light.

WHAT IS THE INTENT AND PURPOSE OF THE ANGELS?

The angels of the Christed One live their lives with the intent and purpose of serving the Christ. They trust whatever is asked of them and they act upon it with their whole existence, never questioning, never doubting their Master. Because of this deep loyalty, the Christ can rely upon them to carry out the tasks that are needed to restore the planet to a state of Light.

THE ANGELIC KINGDOM AND THE HIERARCHY

At this time many of the angels, especially those of Raphael's group, are busy helping to bring forth the Light of Christ and the Spirit of Resurrection in a special blend of energy that will bring forth the new humanity. This will help us on Earth to begin to merge our consciousness with that of the angels, helping us to function simultaneously in the physical plane as well as in the inner worlds. This is a needed Light which will help to change our consciousness and help to transform the planet Earth. The Masters, in particular the Lord Count of Saint Germain (the Master governing the violet Ray or Light) and certain female Masters, are working to assist in this process. We can call on Them to help us make the necessary shifts and transitions which we in our life on Earth must make.

The Lady Portia and the Count of Saint Germain can help us to redeem and transmute our shadow selves, the darker side of our nature. They can help us learn to discriminate and recognise what is shadow and what is Light. They are Masters of alchemy and can help us to separate the darker substance within us, recognise it, acknowledge its source and transmute and release it in the Light, allowing us to change our constitution and turn from darkness to Light.

The Lady Yasodhara can help us find the joy of working and living in the Light. She helps us find compassion for ourselves and others as we walk the Path, giving great wisdom and understanding previously unknown. She is known for Her perseverance; through Her link with the Lord of Love She can help take us home to His Heart. In so doing we find our own hearts and can learn to walk the Way of the Heart. We can call upon Her and Her many angels of golden Light to help us when we need to find the joy, the compassion, the wisdom and the never-ceasing love.

We can call on the Lady Nada and Her host of angels in the pink Light when we wish to help heal those who are sick in body and mind or to help heal the suffering deep within. When we know someone is suffering, we can ask Lady Nada to send a healing angel to be with the person until the healing, in whatever form, is complete. We can call on the Archangel Raphael to send His healing angels to help heal those who are suffering on Earth and to help them find comfort and relief.

There are so many beings we can call upon when we or others around us are in need. The Masters and the Archangels, the angels, and the angels assisting them dedicate themselves to the work of Light. It may be that when we call upon these great beings to assist us that the Masters and Archangels may not come; however, Their assisting angels will do so and will give us the help we need no matter how insignificant we may see ourselves as being, no matter how tiny may be our needs in comparison to the needs of many. The help will be given.

THE FALLEN ANGELS

Some angels have taken the dark path, they are often referred to as the fallen angels. They are the ones who have rebelled against God's Laws. Many religions do not like to even call these dark beings angels. They represent the negative forces whose qualities are vices such as pride, greed, gluttony, lust, jealousy and envy. Some of these forces work to trick and tease human beings in a mischievous and negative manner. These beings are known to be able to change shape and form and exist at varying levels of ability. When we make a choice for darkness instead of Light, there are associated lessons which we only need look into history to learn. Let us look, for example, at Noah's Ark when the great prophet Noah was alerted through God's messages of the dangers if humanity did not change its way. No one would listen and the great floods came. Perhaps now, many centuries later, when the prophets are again warning us, we might listen and make the choice to lift into the realms of the celestial beings rather than follow the downward path of the fallen ones.

We are all prone to being tripped up by our own negative natures. However, we can learn from this how the darkness works, and with practice and determination learn to overcome it, to keep our shadows in check and to strengthen the Light within with the help of the angels of Light. Our choice of working for darkness or for Light is an important one and it is one which we must make regularly in all our interactions and life choices, for the veils of deceit can be strong. We must pray for the help of the angels to help us lift, so that we are not caught in the glamours and illusions which make it so easy for us to fall. When we fall, we must learn to recognise this and acknowledge the truth of this falling. We must stand again and never give up our search for the Light. By our falls we find humility again, which has usually been lost in the glamour. We find truth again which is lost in the illusion, and we are reminded of our place in this mighty universe. We are like grains of sand on the floor of the mighty ocean - nothing; yet when God is within us we are One, we are Everything. We often fall, sometimes through conscious intent and often due to our lack of discrimination. So let us think, "do we wish to continue to fall victim to glamour and illusion, to the lords of deceit, or do we wish to rise with the angels to a world of great Light, love and compassion?" The choice is ours, we can decide. All we need to do is remember to ask the angels to lift us, and they will lift us to the Heart of their Teacher and ours, the Lord of Love. If we really wish to become like them, we can pray to be like them one day, to become one of the shining ones. We will be given help in learning to discriminate and God will hear our prayer and act accordingly.

So how do we discern a true angel when other voices, such as desires of our personality, may interfere? When we decide to live a life based on truth, we open to the spiritual forces. When we open the heart and decide to live a life based on love and truth, we begin to receive attention from greater beings who can utilise us for Light work. It is not until we are cleansed and purified sufficiently that higher powers support us in the work. When the higher forces know that we will use the Light given for good purpose without thought of return, it is then that we can begin to be trusted. If we wish to send Light for certain purposes, we must be open to the Will of God. The work then becomes a suggestion designed to benefit the good of all. Our motivation must be to serve; an impersonal yet heartfelt approach is needed. We ask the Christ-self to overshadow our personality so that we may work impersonally with the Divine.

Psychic phenomena can disrupt good group work. Through it people get caught in glamours and illusions and lose sight of the spiritual purpose and intent. They may talk about these inner experiences in a way that belittles the purity of the experiences and makes them like a grand picture show. When people do this, the work loses its power. This is not to say that such beautiful experiences cannot be shared. It simply means that if it is done in a manner that is self-aggrandising instead of in love and wisdom, it will destroy the beauty and grace of the energies and experience given. In silence and purity of heart much can be done. Where the motive is simply to be a vehicle for the higher Light, the Light can work through us. If we would like to have the help of the angels, we must keep this in mind.

If there is a specific work we wish to achieve, it is good to know that regular activities, for example, at a certain time each day or week, will attract the angels, and an energy of cooperation can build. In all this we must remain forever mindful and be realistic about what can be achieved. We must work with the sense of pride that may come as we work with the angels and guard against self-deceit. If we are to obtain cooperation, we must have clarity of thought and focussed concentration to use the energy given in an efficient and well-directed way. When we understand right use of colour or words we can fine-tune our cooperative efforts. There is a certain greatness of energy and oneness of the human vehicles when we work together in cooperation for the Light.

Certain angels are linked with Divine consciousness. In *The Kingdom of the Gods* Hodson speaks of the Rose Angel, a great angel radiating a beautiful luminous pink Light, which can be thought of as an incarnation of Divine Wisdom and Love. When we get the help of such angels to cooperate in service, it is indeed an honour.

When we work ceremonially, and when we heal, we should do so with the right motive and purity of heart, invoking the Light and Love of the Holy Spirit and the Christ Light, leaving, in full faith, the healing to the higher powers in accordance with the karma of the person being healed. We must put our personal will aside and have no attachment to the outcome. When the healing angels are involved, they will direct their streams of purified energy into and through the aura of the person being healed to disperse congestion and drive out harmful substances.

GUARDIAN ANGELS

Guardian angels have the job of protecting and guarding people and places, giving protection from negativity and keeping a holy space around whatever it is they are guarding. They use their Light body with its forces of Light to create Light around the object in their keeping.

We all have a guardian angel. Our guardian angel may stay with us over many lifetimes, and it strives to cooperate with the will of the soul or the solar angel. Together the solar angel and the guardian angel work to guide us in our evolution. We can come to know our guardian angel as an energy we can trust. Some may feel it, some may communicate through inner symbol. It will speak to us through colour, Light and sound as the angels do.

Our guardian angel works at helping us to strengthen the goodness in our nature. It can warn us when there are dangers, whether they come from the outside or from parts of our own personalities. When we call on it, we can ask it to protect us from the darkness or the fallen angels we spoke of earlier. When we develop a strong communication with our guardian angel, along with the inner trust that brings, we discover that we are not alone and help is at hand.

Our guardian angel has other angels who assist it in its tasks, who may run messages for it, and therefore, for us. As long as we strive to live by the spiritual Law, these angels can help. Our guardian angels are often aware of our karma and may work to help us understand what needs to be understood. They may tell us the next step on our path and can even alert us to negative people or environments we may enter, hinting that we move with caution. They communicate with us at a level we can comprehend. In spiritual circles today many people speak of "the Higher Self," when they are referring to inner guidance they receive. What they are probably really communicating with is the guardian angel whose task it is to guard and guide us on our path. The Higher Self is another term for the soul or solar angel which cannot be contacted readily by us because it is at a level of consciousness that we cannot comprehend - thus, we have the guardian angel to help us. The solar angel can freely contact the guardian angel who finds ways of passing on the message, so to speak.

The relationship you have with your guardian angel is an important one. Like all relationships, if you abuse it in one life, it may be difficult to have a good relationship in the next. There is often a strong karmic link between you and your guardian angel - perhaps you have walked the Earth together at some point. Much karma can be released and learning gained by being a guardian angel to a human being or even to a place such as a waterfall, a mountain, or a tree. Guardian angels are ever ready to shield us from harm. They bring harmony and love and work to keep away all influences of danger, or darkness and disease.

SOLAR ANGELS

The solar angel is a term used for the soul. The solar angels are angels of Light. It is the solar angel who does Light work and through meditation, aspiration and control is able to influence the lower forces and make them its servants. When we wish to achieve positive Light work, we can work with our solar angels to achieve our positive ends. When we heal and call upon the soul, the solar angel becomes active and sends the Light needed to assist in the healing work.

There are solar angels of the planetary scheme and of the solar system, but here we are focussing on the solar angel of individuals. The solar angel, or the soul, transforms the Light from the highest levels of consciousness to a vibration that we can bear. If we are healing and do not wish to bring too much energy down, we know we can rely on the solar angel, as well as the guardian angel, to keep the healing at a vibration with which the client can cope. This ensures that the healing takes place according to the karma of the individual and the Will of God. Solar angels work as the great builders putting life force into form. Guardian angels hold this Light given by the solar angels and act as way-showers, shining the Light for us as we walk our path. The solar angels and their great work is here very simply described. If you wish to pursue a deeper understanding of them, you may refer to Alice Bailey's book *A Treatise of Cosmic Fire*.

Hodson in *Kingdom of the Gods* tells us that studying the angels on an individual basis sometimes brings confusion. They so often work in groups and are a conscious part of the one pulsating universe. When we try to understand their work, we do so lacking their consciousness and so can easily misinterpret their work by comparing it too much with individual human life patterns. The angels are able to show us, through their example, the possibilities of how our lives can one day be. When we cooperate with each other, we can help each other to evolve. The solar angels are aware of the higher scheme. The guardian angels work to convey to us what we need to know in order to work and cooperate with that higher scheme.

The angels' purpose is to serve the Christ. They know how to serve and display the virtues of faith, trust and loyalty which we so need to learn. There are hundreds of virtues which the angels embody, and if we need help to develop just one of them, we can call upon the angel of that virtue. In this chapter we have looked at the angels in the grand scheme of the universe and have seen how they also help in the process of our daily life with what may seem like small things, which nonetheless assist us in creating a smooth and harmonious flow to our lives. Let us remember to call on them for the help they can give. Let us open our hearts to them and let them teach us what it is to relax and trust. Listen for their message, whether it comes through Light, colour or symbol, or as a beautiful feeling in our heart, and learn to fly with them so we can experience the freedom and liberation of Spirit which they bring.

THE DEVAS ON THE SEVEN RAYS

On the Seven Rays there are angels who bring the colour of that Ray and work with it. These angels are often referred to as devas. The Seven Rays are Great Beings sending streams of Great Holy Light that contain particular qualities. When a Ray energy is needed to do particular work, for example, the violet Ray to transmute, we can call upon the devas of the violet Light to help with the process of transmutation; or if purification is required, the devas of the blue and white Light may be called to help with cleansing and purification.

The violet devas are associated with the building of the etheric doubles; the green devas preside over the magnetic spots of the Earth, guarding the forests and defending them from interference. It is from these groups at a certain stage in their evolution that some guardian angels are chosen. The violet devas educate human beings in the perfecting of the physical body.

The white devas can be called upon to help us purify. Alice A. Bailey, in *A Treatise on Cosmic Fire*, tells that there are white devas of the air and water who preside over the atmosphere and work with certain aspects of electrical phenomena, controlling the seas, the rivers and the streams. Alice Bailey[29] also tells us that the path of service for the green devas is in their work of magnetisation and protection of the vegetable kingdom and of sacred places of Earth, and that the path of service for the white devas lies in the guarding of individuals within the human kingdom and the control of air and water elementals. Through this work these devas can themselves evolve, just as we can, through our service for the Christ.

FORGIVENESS

Many of us feel unworthy of receiving help, and we find it difficult to forgive ourselves of real and imagined errors. Perhaps we have realised our own negativity. It is difficult then in the shadow to open to the Light of the angels and to feel deserving of it. Our lack of self-worth acts as a barrier to our letting in the Light; however, it is in these darker moments that we need the help of the angels the most. We need to remind ourselves to call upon them in our times of inner crisis. We can call upon the Angel of Forgiveness to forgive ourselves and to forgive others. The Angel of Forgiveness can appear as a white, light violet or pink angel. It has magnificent Forces of Light that pour from its heart, through its wings which gently work on and transmute our grievance and replaces it with love.

When you call upon the Angel of Forgiveness, you can visualise the light violet Light coming down from its heart, through the Angels' wings into your heart centre; allow the violet Light to gently release the grievance you are holding onto about a situation or a person or yourself. In *The Living*

Word of the Hierarchy, Ananda Tara Shan[30] writes about the Law of Forgiveness:

> *The Law of Forgiveness must be understood and then invoked in every situation where the shadow self has made chaos and destruction. It is through that Law that you learn to laugh, to be gentle, to be just, and to act with wisdom learned from making numerous mistakes. Invoke the Law and become Master of your own destiny.*
>
> *Do it this way:*
>
> *Law of Forgiveness, Mercy of God, I have erred. I have learned my lesson. Descend into . . . . (the problem), and neutralise the negative substance created by my actions, replacing it with the loving Light of Tara the White.*

The White Tara, the Mother Christ, shines Her great Light upon us as an Avatar of Light and helps us to face ourselves. She accepts us and will take our shadow and lift it when we call upon Her, taking it in as a mother would take in a tiny child. She gives us the nourishment we need and the courage to see ourselves in truth. In Her Light and the Light of the Lady Portia, Lady Nada and Lady Yasodhara, we can find forgiveness.

When we visualise the Light of Forgiveness, we can see it as light violet Light entering into our heart. We can see the hearts of those we forgive radiating with pink Light, allowing the white Light to purify the link between us. We can see how this Light helps all of our relationships move into Light.

The angels are increasingly working to make themselves known to us. Why? Because they can help us lift our consciousness and so help the Earth to lift and become a planet of Light in a Lighted Universe. When we heal, the angels are at hand, ever ready to help us and to lift the burdens and sorrow from our stilted paths. The angels help us to raise our awareness to the Lighted Path which we can find within us. If we dare to follow it and fly with them into the Light, we can begin to live in Love.

a

CALL TO ACTION

A CALL TO ACTION

Humanity and the planet Earth are in a state of crisis. There are seven sacred planets in our solar system and Earth is not one of them. In order for Earth to be lifted to become a star of light, which is its destiny, we on Earth need to change our ways, to transform and heal our lower nature so that we can raise the vibration of Earth and ourselves to a higher level. We can learn a great deal from the angels and can strive to lift our vibration and become more like them. To see the truth of ourselves is not always easy, especially when so many of us have invested so much time and energy into denying the existence of our shadow. The angels by their light-hearted and loving nature are able to assist us in the process of working through and dealing with our lower natures. They help us see the Light and lift to see things from a higher level. The angels are one with the inner worlds and with their help we can learn how the inner worlds function. Unlike us they are not bound to Earth by their physical bodies and can move freely in the world of Light. They help bring revelation, insight, faith, hope, forgiveness and healing, helping us restore our trust and helping us open to higher vision with God. They work with colour, Light and symbol, strengthen virtues of goodness and help us sanctify ourselves. The angels open to us a world where peace and joy abide. Through the Light, colour and symbols they send we come to know them as the messengers of God. They can bring the humour of the creative intelligence and use sharp mind and wit to help us understand the messages we are given. If we truly wish to rise into the Light of the Higher Mind where they live, we should call on them and they can lift us. They can help us to see ourselves, our strengths and our weaknesses. When we encroach upon the spiritual Laws they make us aware of the impurity of our acts so that we can take ourselves in check and rectify our negative actions.

As said earlier, there are angels that look after trees, mountains, lakes and land masses. The angels look after the Earth and nature generally. If we care to attune to these devas we will find our conscience and discover whether our acts are in alignment with the Divine Will or not. But to hear the angels we need to be prepared to stop and listen and act upon the guidance they give us. If we have made an error we can ask the angels to help us find out how to make up for that error by asking them what we should do. For example, I once had a friend who had chopped down trees which stressed greatly the tree deva of that region. Because it was an earnest mistake which he truly wished to rectify from his heart, he asked for forgiveness from the tree deva and asked what he could do to make up for his error that could help the plant kingdom. The guidance was given that he was to cut no more trees down, instead he was to plant a particular number of trees in the same region. There are many other stories where people have disturbed rock spirits through positioning their houses without thought of the lay of the land. Often people are unaware of the karma that comes from such thoughtlessness. However, if they wake up and realise from the heart the mistake through ignorance and take responsibility for this, it is often not too late to find a way to give back to the Earth what has been taken. But if we look at the Earth on a national level, we see how far humanity has gotten out of hand and how little care is given to the forests, to the Earth generally and we see how materialism and greed have taken over.

To truly listen takes courage and willingness to face ourselves and change our ways. Often people discover and know in their hearts what is needed but neglect to do so and have many wonderful excuses for their neglect. At some point humanity needs to stop, listen, act and rectify damages done. That point has come.

As was noted earlier, it is part of the Plan of the coming New Age that human and angelic consciousness blend, and create a new humanity. The new humanity are known as the Children of the Heart, children of the Lord Maitreya, Who is the Lord of the Heart. The new humanity is one that will respond to the Teachings of the Heart. The Teachings of the Heart are the Laws and teachings for the Children of the Heart, given by the Christ as a way of life. These Teachings teach the way of the universal brother-sisterhood and act as a guide to help humanity live by the heart. They are also known as the Doctrine of the Heart. The Children of the Heart will strive to embody and live by the principles that are taught in these Teachings.

It is an enormous grace that certain Masters (great Beings who have walked the Path before us) and Archangels are working together with the Lord Christ, who is the Lord of Love, Maitreya, the Teacher of angels and humanity, to help us in the process of merging our consciousness with that of the angels. With Their help the veil can be lifted and we may become one with the angelic kingdom and awaken our consciousness to that of the angels. To show our love for the Christ, and to open to this process, we must begin by learning to love each other, and by learning to love and respect the Earth and nature. We must also open to our angelic helpers to help light the way. In so doing we come to live in balance and harmony with each other on the Earth. These are the first steps. Only by taking them can we begin to become the new humanity. In deciding to live by the heart we can begin to prepare for the coming of the Lord Maitreya in 500 years.

REFERENCES

ARCHANGELS

Blavatsky, H.P. (1963). The Secret Doctrine Volume 1. Pasedena, California: Theosophical University Press.

Davidson, G. (1967). A Dictionary of Angels: including the fallen angels. New York: The Free Press.

Heline, C. (1993). Stargates. California: New Age on Philosophy centre.

Luk, A. D. (1960). Law of Life II. Okalahoma: Luk Publications.

Metford, J.C.J. (1983). Dictionary of Christian Lore and Legend. London: Thames and Hudson.

Wilson, P.L. (1980). Angels. London: Thames and Hudson.

ANGELS

Ananda Tara Shan (1993). The Living Word of the Hierarchy. Daylesford, Victoria: Maitreya Surya Publishing House.

Bailey, A. A. (1982). A Treatise on Cosmic Fire. New York: Lucis Publishing Co.

Davidson, G. (1967). A Dictionary of Angels: including the fallen Angels. New York: The Free Press.

Hodson, G. (1987). The Kingdom of the Gods. Madras: Vasanta Press.

Hodson, G. (1988). The Brotherhood of Angels and Men. Illinois: Theosophical Publishing House.

Hodson, G. Angels and the New Race. Out of print.

Wyllie, T. (1992). Ask your Angels. New York: Ballantine Books.

ENDNOTES

1   Heline, *Stargates.*
2   Blavatsky, *The Secret Doctrine Volume 1,* 28.
3   Hodson, *The Kingdom of the Gods,* 53.
4   Blavatsky, 246.
5   Bible, *The New Testament 1971.*
6   Heline.
7   Ibid.
8   Wilson, *Angels.*
9   Heline.
10   Luk, *Law of Life II.*
11   Heline.
12   Bible, *New Testament, Matthew 5 - 7.*
13   Ibid., *Enoch 1, 10: 1-3.*
14   Heline.
15   Ibid.
16   Ibid.
17   Ibid., 167.
18   Ibid., 48.
19   Ibid., 59.
20   Ibid., 85.
21   Ibid., 93.
22   Ibid., 88.
23   Heline.
24   Ibid., 143.
25   Ibid., 139.
26   Bible, *The New Testament, Matthew 5-7, 1971,*
        Revised Standard Version: Collins
27   Hodson, *The Kingdom of the Gods,* 158.
28   Ibid.
29   Bailey, *A Treatise on Cosmic Fire.*
30   Ananda Tara Shan, *The Living Word of the Hierarchy,* 59.

INDEX

H

I

J

K

L

M

PUBLICATIONS

Deva Wings Publications was formed on Right Human Relations Day in 1994.

Its purpose and objectives are:

1. to spread the Light by creating literature and other materials that help us to understand Spirit and make the teachings of Theosophy (Divine Wisdom) comprehensible to all.

2. to educate people in the theosophical principles.

3. to educate people in spiritual psychology so that we may come to understand ourselves and become that which we truly are.

Deva is a Sanskrit word meaning shining one or angel. The concept is such that the Light and teachings of Spirit will spread over the Earth on the devas' wings.

ABOUT TARAJYOTI GOVINDA
(1958-1999)

B.A. Dip. Ed. Grad Dip. Psych. Couns. MAPS

After a spiritual awakening and death experience in 1983, Tara began working as a spiritual healer, counsellor, teacher and group facilitator. She became a psychologist whose major focus was the synthesis of spiritual and psychological transformation. Tarajyoti was the founder and director of The Transformational College of Education and co-founder and director of The Theosophical School of Healing.

Her main interests were Theosophy (the study of Divine Wisdom); Jungian psychology; music; native spirituality; being in nature; painting and other creative endeavours.

Tarajyoti ascended 5 April 1999 after many years of devoted work.

PUBLICATIONS

We have a range of:

- Books
- E-books
- Audio Books
- Meditations

available at
WWW.DEVAWINGS.COM

The Healing Hands of Love
a guide to spiritual healing

Tarajyoti Govinda

THE HEALING HANDS OF LOVE:

A GUIDE TO SPIRITUAL HEALING

The Healing Hands of Love is a journey into the spiritual realms, delivering a blend of spiritual knowledge and wisdom that comes from experience and heart.

This book is written as a guide for those walking the spiritual path. It contains heartfelt tales of communion with Spirit intertwined with the Divine Wisdom.

A vast array of spiritual topics are covered, including: spiritual healing; the angels; the human structure; the chakras; the aura and its colours; the healer; reincarnation; karma; the unconscious; regression; guided imagery; alchemy and healing the shadow.

The Healing Hands of Love is for those who wish to heal.

paperback, 338 pages

BECOMING WHOLE:

THE PSYCHOLOGY OF LIGHT

In this book Tarajyoti addresses the issue of Spirit in our psychology, taking us through the wastelands to the Grail of our heart, reminding us of the healing power of love and Light.

Becoming Whole takes us on a journey towards the lightness of being; creating alchemy; discovering our many selves; empowering the higher mind; looking for meaning; embodying the dream; meeting the monster; taking courage; finding forgiveness; sharing from the heart; trusting in immortality and embracing the Grail.

It is for all who seek to know themselves and aspire to acquaint themselves with the Light of soul. It is a guide for self-exploration which provides some of the keys we need for dealing with our anger, fears, guilt, grief and depression and for opening to the Light within our being.

paperback, 339 pages

The Joy of
Enlightenment

Tarajyoti Govinda

THE JOY OF ENLIGHTENMENT

"When our hearts begin to fill with compassion we are unaware of what sweet miracles may come. Life changes. Motives change. Our senses are touched and a softening occurs. Sometimes tears flow. There is no pity. No condescension. There is a consciousness that embraces all with love."

The Joy of Enlightenment follows the story of the Lord Gautama Buddha from his princely upbringing, through his renunciation of all worldly goods, to his enlightment under the Bodhi tree and beyond.

This book also looks at Lord Buddha's teachings which include the Four Noble Truths and The Eightfold Path. These teachings can guide us on our own path to enlightenment.

paperback, 154 pages

The Language Of The Heart
Is Spoken All Over The World

Tara Govinda-Rose

THE LANGUAGE OF THE HEART:

IS SPOKEN ALL OVER THE WORLD

In this book Tarajyoti confronts the shadow which so often prevents us from listening to the language of the heart. She explores her life, both present and past, which she is awakened to through a near-death experience. She takes us with her on a journey into the spiritual worlds where communion with the inner self is established.

This spiritual journey outlines the joys and tests that challenge us as we walk the spiritual path. You are taken on a journey through the Himalayas, through the dark night of the soul to the Light that comes from such a journey.

It will touch your heart and awaken you to the depths of your own journey on the path towards Love and Light.

paperback, 146 pages

CPSIA information can be obtained
at www.ICGtesting.com
Printed in the USA
FSOW04n1256100715
8757FS